Praise for *The Inescapable Presence*:

I am so pleased to have this opportunity to say a word of introduction about Cheryl Edris. I have known Cheryl for many years now and I am thrilled to see that she has put her love for the Lord and interest in His Word into a devotional book to help others learn and grow. 'The Inescapable Presence' is a fine devotional book that I am sure you will enjoy. Cheryl has taken material that for many can be quite difficult and has made it easy for even beginners to understand. She has infused each devotional with so much of her own personality that reading it is like sitting down and talking to her about the scriptures. Through reading and working this devotional daily, you will get a sense of Cheryl's love of the book of Genesis and her desire that you get as much out of this study as she has.

—Pastor Dave Terhune
Park Place Wesleyan Church
Pinellas Park, FL

Through life experiences, Cheryl has experienced the comfort of a relationship with God. Recognizing that the Bible is part of the conversation God has with His children, she has recorded some of God's wisdom and counsel she discovered in the book of Genesis. Knowing God's Word is both timeless and timely, she shares it with the reader to comfort and to edify.

—Jan Warner
Facilitator in Women's Ministries

This Study of the Book of Genesis provides the reader with an excellent combination of commentary and resource. But, what value are facts without application. The word "study" in the sub-title and "trials" in the introduction tip us off that here is a book of fifty-five lessons filled with insight and application for daily living.

I heartily recommend this book for personal study and edification. Also, with the need of good Small Group materials today and the addition of a few discussion questions, this book could serve as a valuable resource and guide for group study.

I am pleased to endorse this study not only because I believe it is an excellent work, but because of its author. It has been my privilege to serve as the author's pastor the last few years. She is a woman of integrity, faith, patience, and unusual Biblical insight as the study in this book will reveal. I commend these pages to the reader's edification and spiritual maturity.

—Rev. Duane C. Seitz, Senior Pastor
Lakeview Wesleyan Church
Marion, Indiana

The Inescapable Presence

A Study of Genesis

Cheryl D. Edris

The Inescapable Presence
A Study of Genesis

Tate Publishing & Enterprises

Published by Tate Publishing & Enterprises, LLC
127 E. Trade Center Terrace | Mustang, Oklahoma 73064 USA
1.888.361.9473 | www.tatepublishing.com

Tate Publishing is committed to excellence in the publishing industry. The company reflects the philosophy established by the founders, based on Psalm 68:11,
"The Lord gave the word and great was the company of those who published it."

Book design copyright © 2009 by Tate Publishing, LLC. All rights reserved.
Cover design by Tyler Evans
Interior design by Stefanie Rooney

Published in the United States of America

ISBN: 978-1-60799-973-7
1. Religion, Biblical Studies, Old Testament
2. Religion, Christian Life, General
09.09.11

Dedication

This study of the lessons learned in the Book of Genesis is dedicated to my family.

A major part of life is learning that we need each other, not only when going through trials but also when enjoying the blessings of God.

May we always seek his counsel and stay close to him and close to each other.

Acknowledgments

First, I want to acknowledge God for giving us his Word and the desire to learn from it.

Second, I want to acknowledge my husband, Gerald, for his help and encouragement in writing this book. When I was searching for a word or a way to express an idea, he was there to help. It was he who encouraged me to seek publication of this study.

Third, I want to acknowledge my family for their love and support when finding out that Mom was going to be a published author.

Last, acknowledgment needs to be given to all those who have spiritually affected my life through the years. These people include family, friends, coworkers, pastors, evangelists, teachers, and others whom God has put within my path. We never know how much influence we have on another's life.

Table of Contents

Foreword   17

Introduction   19

Lesson 1: The Lesson of Sovereignty   25
    Who's in Charge Anyway?

Lesson 2: The Lesson of Presence   27
    The Garden of Eden

Lesson 3: The Lesson of Punishment   29
    The Fall of Man

Lesson 4: The Lesson of Jealousy   32
    Cain and Abel

Lesson 5: The Lesson of the Importance of Life   35
    The Generations of Adam

Lesson 6: The Lesson of Preservation   38
    The Flood

Lesson 7: The Lesson of Obedience   41
    The Ark and the Flood

Lesson 8: The Lesson of Remembrance   44
    The Landing of the Ark

Lesson 9: The Lesson of Promises   47
    God's Covenant

Lesson 10: The Lesson of Heritage   50
    The Lists of Names

Lesson 11: The Lesson of Pride   53
    The Tower of Babel

Lesson 12: The Lesson of Mortality   55
    From Shem to Abram

Lesson 13: The Lesson of Trust   58
    The Call of Abram

Lesson 14: The Lesson of Fear   61
    Abram Lies about Sarai

Lesson 15: The Lesson of Decision-Making   64
    Abram and Lot Separate

Lesson 16: The Lesson of God's Care   67
    Abram Rescues Lot

Lesson 17: The Lesson of Prophecy   70
    God's Covenant with Abram

Lesson 18: The Lesson of "Helping God"   73
    Hagar and Ishmael

Lesson 19: The Lesson of Confirmation   77
    The Covenant of Circumcision

Lesson 20: The Lessons of Recognition and Mercy   80
    The Three Visitors

Lesson 21: The Lessons of Protection and Judgment   83
    Sodom and Gomorrah Destroyed

Lesson 22: The Lesson of Looking Ahead   87
    Lot's Wife and the Pillar of Salt

Lesson 23: The Lesson of Influence   90
    Lot and His Daughters

Lesson 24: The Lesson of Responding to Truth   94
    Abraham and Abimelech

Lesson 25: The Lesson of Laughter   97
    Isaac Is Born

Lesson 26: The Lesson of Letting Go and Letting God   101
    Hagar and Ishmael Sent Away

Lesson 27: The Lesson of Making Agreements   104
    Treaty at Beersheba

Lesson 28: The Lesson of Faithfulness   108
    Abraham Tested

Lesson 29: The Lesson of Integrity   111
    The Death of Sarah

Lesson 30: The Lesson of Testimony   114
    Isaac and Rebekah

Lesson 31: The Lesson of Passing the Torch   117
    The Death of Abraham

Lesson 32: The Lesson of Costly Decisions   120
    Jacob and Esau

Lesson 33: The Lesson of Hindsight   123
    Isaac and Abimelech

Lesson 34: The Lesson of Deceitfulness   127
    Jacob Gets Isaac's Blessing

Lesson 35: The Lesson of Time   131
    Jacob Flees to Laban

Lesson 36: The Lesson of Finding Bethel   133
    Jacob's Dream

Lesson 37: The Lesson of God's Hand   135
    Jacob's Marriage

Lesson 38: The Lesson of One-Upmanship   138
    Jacob's Children

Lesson 39: The Lesson of Consequences   141
    Jacob Flees from Laban

Lesson 40: The Lesson of Preparedness   144
    Jacob Prepares to Meet Esau

Lesson 41: The Lesson of Encountering   147
    Jacob Wrestles with God

Lesson 42: The Lesson That God Goes Before   150
    Jacob Meets Esau

Lesson 43: The Lesson of Home   154
    Dinah and the Shechemites;
        Jacob Returns to Bethel

Lesson 44: The Lesson of the Importance of Recognition   158
    Esau's Descendants

Lesson 45: The Lesson That God Is in Control   161
    The Dreamer Is Sold

Lesson 46: The Lesson to Do Justly   166
    Judah and Tamar

Lesson 47: The Lesson of Faithfulness to God   169
    The Dreamer Is Imprisoned

Lesson 48: The Lesson of Waiting   173
    The Dreamer Is Remembered

Lesson 49: The Lesson of Leadership   177
    The Dreamer Is Rewarded

Lesson 50: The Lesson of Honesty   181
    The Dreamer Is Avenged

Lesson 51: The Lesson of Forgiveness and Restoration   186
    The Dream Is Fulfilled; The Truth Is Exposed

Lesson 52: The Lesson of Answered Prayer   190
    The Family Moves to Egypt

Lesson 53: The Lesson of a Father's Blessing   193
    Jacob's Final Years

Lesson 54: The Lesson of Leaving a Legacy   196
    The Burial of Jacob; The Death of Joseph

Lesson 55: The Lesson of a Second Look   199
    Heritage, Take Two

Final Thoughts   203

Foreword

"Bible study" has a variety of meanings in our world today. It ranges from college professors engaged in scholarly analysis of a passage to several junior high teens sharing what they think a verse means in a Sunday School class. There are scholars who spend a lifetime learning the Biblical languages in order to provide us with all the subtle shades of meaning in the words we read. Biblical archeologists go on digs to uncover historical and cultural background to enrich the text. Theologians go for big-picture ideas that trace the shaping of Christian doctrine through the centuries of the Biblical story.

God's primary purpose in giving us his Word was not for scholarly analysis and theological debate; it was for transformation of our lives. The best insights from scripture come from those who have lived with Scripture and allowed its message to alter their attitudes and actions. In this stroll through the book of Genesis, Cheryl Edris does not look under every rock and behind every tree to point out every little detail of the text. Instead she pauses only for a few moments to point out a key life application found in each chapter. She rarely uses her own experiences to tell us how to live, instead she lets the characters in this ancient story provide the lessons we can and should learn in order to walk with God. Her wisdom comes from the Holy Spirit, the teacher who guides us into truth and her classroom has been the experiences and trials that are common to all those who devote themselves to God and simple service to others.

Walk through the book of Genesis with her. Pluck the "fruit of the Spirit" from these verses and in doing so you will "grow in grace and in the knowledge of our Lord and Savior, Jesus Christ."

—Dr. Bud Bence
Ph.D. - Historical Theology - Emory University
Professor of Church History
Indiana Wesleyan University

Introduction

We have all faced times when it seemed things could not get worse, those times when:

- your marriage is falling apart.
- the kids are constantly in trouble.
- your husband or wife just died.
- your child has an incurable disease.
- you have cancer.
- your parents are getting a divorce.
- you lost your job.
- you lost everything in a fire or flood or storm.
- you or someone you know is in a downward spiral from which there seems to be no escape.

Trials can be personal, emotional, positional, and financial. They can happen to people we do not know, to people we love, and to us. There are trials that could have been prevented had we learned from experience, planned better, or used common sense; and there are inescapable trials it seems we have to go through at some time in our lives, trials of illness and death.

When I first met my husband, Gerald, my mother was in the hospital dying with cancer. Gerald's sister was a nurse at the hospital, and she arranged a "blind date" for us to meet. The night Gerald came to meet me, my mom was on the verge of death with pneumonia. Our meeting was brief. He invited me out for a soda, but I told him I could not leave that night, maybe another time. Through excellent nursing skills, his sister saved my mother's life that night. Beyond that, however, this wonderful nurse had introduced me to my future husband.

Gerald did call me sometime later for a date. It seemed we always met at the hospital or stopped by there sometime when we were together. Gerald's aunt and uncle had both recently died of cancer, so Gerald knew somewhat what I was going through watching my mom die. I was nineteen years old and a sophomore in college at the time. I spent most of my "free time" at the hospital with my mom, doing homework at her bedside and trying to help her as best I could. My dad and I stayed with an aunt and uncle in the city so we would be closer to the hospital in case of an emergency. I commuted to a college about forty miles away.

Gerald and I fell in love at first sight; and after only about five weeks of dating, he asked me to marry him. It was on a Sunday. My mom had not eaten for several days. We stopped by the hospital to see her before we left for the day. She was hungry! I remember feeding her raspberry sherbet and her wanting a second small serving. She ate that too! We left encouraged, yet wondering if this was her getting better before she would become worse.

Gerald and I had a lovely Sunday afternoon

together, and during that time, he proposed and I accepted. We stopped back at the hospital later that day to tell my mom the good news. She had lapsed into a coma and died the following Saturday morning. I never had the opportunity to tell her that Gerald and I were going to be married.

My mom and I were very close. She was more than my mom; she was my best friend. It was difficult to watch her become worse and worse over the brief six months she had from the time the cancer was discovered. I learned how to give her shots for nausea and vomiting. I took her for treatments on days I had college classes and arranged for her to have a place to stay until classes were done. I tried to talk to her when communication seemed almost impossible. And I saw her grow closer and closer to the Lord.

After talking to her cousin a few months before, mom had rededicated her life to God. From that time on, one could see the change and growth in her faith. That assurance of her destination of heaven made the times of suffering more bearable for all of us. I was strong for her and for my dad. I was strong for everyone at the funeral. But when all that was over, I wept; and God comforted me.

I so wanted to tell my mom about Gerald and I getting married, but I am sure she already knew that. She had met Gerald at the hospital and knew him from the month of visits. She liked him! I am sure she was happy for me and was glad Gerald would be there to help me through the days ahead.

Life is sometimes very wonderful and sometimes very difficult. Gerald bought me an engagement ring and gave it to me the weekend after mom's funeral. We were engaged on Friday the thirteenth! We were married one year later, on Saturday the thirteenth! Our first year of marriage was wonderful, but the inescapable trial of death persisted. During that year of dating and our first year of marriage, we lost nine family members, including my mom, Gerald's dad, both of our grandmothers, and aunts and uncles. We were to the point of never wanting to see a funeral home again!

But God, he was there. He became real to us. He loved us. He brought us through. He brought Gerald and me together when we needed each other the most.

Oh yes, over our thirty-nine years of marriage, we have had many trials, including another inescapable trial: the loss of health.

Gerald was a mechanic when we met. I do believe he must have had a wrench in his hand the day he was born! He and his brother, Max, spent many, many hours helping their dad work on cars and tractors in their family garage. They kept their own vehicles and machinery going as well as helped many friends in their rural farming community. Gerald did heavy engine work and was known for his expertise in his field of engine repair, whether car, tractor, or semi. However, after three years of marriage, he ruptured a disc in his back and was unable to work. By this time, we had one child, one child on the way, a house, and no other income. Once again, we were facing an inescapable trial. Gerald had numerous tests and ultimately had three back surgeries, one every two years for six years. His back was better, but the pain has been there most of the time since then. Now, after more procedures and more surgeries, he is disabled, has to take several medications, and has a neurostimulator implant to help with pain control.

But God—oh, but God has taken care of us. As I look back over our lifetime together, I can see where God intervened, leading us to just the right doctor at just the right time. He blessed us with a wonderful family. In our mid-thirties, he called us into ministry, and Gerald became the oldest student in his college class (graduating with honors, I might add)! Gerald was able to pastor twenty years before the degenerative disc disease and back pain made it impossible for him to work anymore. God has taught us through these trials, and we continue to depend on him. We have learned, and we continue to learn as we continue through life.

The inescapable presence of God—he is there; he loves us and wants to help us. Unfortunately, sometimes it seems we have to be flat on our backs with problems and trials before we can look up and seek God.

As I thought through some of the trials we have faced, I was reminded of the people in the Book of Genesis. What lessons did these people learn from their trials? What lessons are there for us to learn? How did God build his people? My curiosity was sparked, and I wanted to identify these lessons learned by God's people in the Book of Genesis.

Thus became this journey, this self-study of this wonderful Book of History. May you discover these lessons and may they help you as you go through your trials. Remember, when it seems like there is no escape, God is there. He is that inescapable presence.

Lesson 1: The Lesson of Sovereignty

Who's in Charge Anyway? (Genesis 1)

"In the beginning God ... "

Genesis 1:1

He speaks and all creation listens!

And God said, "Let there be light" and there was day and night. "Let there be an expanse between the waters" and there was sky. "Let there be land and seas and let the land produce vegetation" and so it was. "Let there be lights in the sky" and the sun and moon and stars appeared. "Let there be living creatures in the sea and birds in the air" and both the seas and air were filled. "Let there be living creatures on the land" and it was so! Ahh, then God said, "Let us make man in our image, in our likeness" so God created man and breathed into him the breath of life.

Genesis 1:3–31

And then God rested! And there was quiet!

The Lesson of Sovereignty

God spoke, and all creation listened and came to be. God is sovereign. He is in charge. He but utters a word, and it comes to pass. He is above all and over all and in all. He has the absolute right to do whatever he sees fit in the world and in our lives. He can see beyond our present trials and guide us through them if we but hold on to him. "And all things work together" for our good if we but trust this lesson of sovereignty.

Oh, Lord, help us to remember that you have supreme power. Help us to allow you controlling influence, guidance, and direction in our lives. Help us to remember that the great I AM, the Alpha and Omega, the Beginning and the End, the Triune God (Father, Son, and Holy Spirit), God Almighty... stepped out of nowhere, onto nothing, spoke but a word, and created everything! You are sovereign.

Questions to Ponder ...

- What do you notice about the order of God's creation? How would you describe it?

- Considering the fact that God created day and night, sun and moon, light and dark, and land and seas, what affect does this truth have on the existence of heaven and hell? Of being saved and being lost?

- What is the difference between "creating" something and "discovering" something? How does this difference affect our beliefs and our lives?

Lesson 2: The Lesson of Presence

The Garden of Eden (Genesis 2)

Have you ever had those times when you feel all alone, like there is no one who cares, no one to whom you can talk, and no one to help you or protect you? It is in those times that we need to remember the lesson of presence.

How can we understand or visualize the presence of God with Adam and Eve in the Garden of Eden—having him walking beside me and talking to me, sitting down beside me in the cool grass by the peaceful waters and listening to the songs of the birds and enjoying the beauty of the flowers, God, himself, in my very presence and me in his presence?

We cannot experience the presence of God in the same way as Adam and Eve experienced it. Sin ruined that! Sin separated us from God's physical presence; sin destroyed the peace of God's presence in the Garden.

But God—

God, who is sovereign, did not withdraw his presence from us. Through Jesus Christ and the Holy Spirit, we can still walk in God's presence, sit beside him, talk to him, listen to him, love him—experience his presence. Yes, he is with us always—even "to the very end of the age" (Matthew 28:20b).

The Lesson of Presence

We, as God's creation, need to realize that we are important to God. He desires our communication with him as much as we need his presence with us. Take time to read his letter to us, the Bible. Take time to talk to him as friend to friend in prayer. Realize he is with us wherever we are in whatever we are doing. We can talk to him while driving down the road, working on an assembly line, changing a diaper, running a race, or sitting by a loved one in a hospital room. God knows us and loves us. He wants to be present in our lives, and he wants us to worship him and make him a part of our lives. He wants to put his loving arms around us and give us peace.

Oh, Lord, help us to desire your presence. Help us to seek your presence. Help us to enjoy your presence, and help us to do so daily.

Questions to Ponder ...

- How do you experience God's presence?

- Do you have a memory of a special time when you knew you were in the presence of God? Share this memory with others.

- Do Christians have times in their lives when they cannot "feel" God's presence?

The Fall of Man (Genesis 3)

With blessings come responsibilities. Adam and Eve were responsible for taking care of the Garden of Eden and all that the Lord God had given them. Adam named all the animals. Can you imagine that? Think of the closeness Adam had to have with God in order to possess the wisdom to be able to name all the animals! His mind and spirit had to have been one with God's.

Then think of God's love for Adam when he created a helper for Adam in the person of woman: Eve. God loved Adam so much that he created a loving relationship for Adam that would introduce marriage and family to all of mankind!

But our God-given gift of choice gave way to poor judgment, and Eve fell to the serpent's deceitful schemes—and sin entered the world and the lives of mankind! We disobeyed God, and thus began the lesson of punishment.

Punishment for disobedience is hard; the ultimate punishment for sin is death! When we disobey what we are told or what we know to be right, we will be punished. Yes, we may try to hide just like Adam and Eve, but we will be found. The truth always comes out, and there will always be consequences that we must face because of our disobedience.

The Lesson of Punishment

Loving parents discipline their children. No, they do not beat them, abandon them, or kill them. Loving parents teach their children the difference between right and wrong. They teach them good manners and respect for others. They teach them to share, to be kind to others, to clean their rooms, to respect authority, and to obey rules. Loving parents discipline their children when they disobey because loving parents love their children.

Have you ever heard a parent about to spank his or her child say, "This is going to hurt me more than it hurts you"? When one is on the receiving end of the punishment, this statement seems absurd! If you are the parent, however, there is a heartfelt emotional pain that tears at your being when you need to punish your child. We are proud of our children; we want them to be healthy and happy. We want the best for them. Our Heavenly Father wants the best for us, too. But, like any child, there are times when we need to be punished for our disobedience.

Oh, Lord, help us to obey your words, your teaching, and your commands. Help us to practice obedience so we need not experience punishment but rather enjoy your blessing.

Questions to Ponder ...

- As a parent, can you share a time when it was difficult to punish your child?

- As a child, can you share a time when you felt you were wrongly punished but realized later it was for your good?

- In what other instances in the Scriptures does God punish his children?

- Does God still punish his children today?

Cain and Abel (Genesis 4)

Brothers and sisters equal playing together, sharing secrets, having fun. However, they also equal times of quarrels and arguments; tricks and lies; and hurts, anger, and jealousy.

Thus was the story of Cain and Abel, two brothers who grew up together but had different likes and talents, much like those of us today. Not everyone in the same family has the same gifts and talents. Everyone is different. Praise the Lord! God has made each of us unique, and in our own ways and with our own talents we can worship him.

But in the case of Cain, jealousy and anger entered the world. Cain thought God liked Abel better; and Cain let those feelings of jealousy, anger, and bitterness build until they led to him killing his brother! I wonder, was it Abel's relationship with God that upset Cain so much, or was it Cain's lack of a relationship with God that caused his jealousy?

Either way, this jealousy and anger split a family then and continues to split the world today!

The Lesson of Jealousy

Jealousy is the root of envy and covetousness. It goes beyond one neighbor wanting to keep up with the other neighbor. A person can be jealous for possessions, position, popularity, and power. One can be jealous of a complete stranger, a personal friend, or a family member. In Galatians 5:19–21, the Apostle Paul tells us that jealousy is an "act of the sinful nature" and "that those who live like this will not inherit the kingdom of God." Jealousy can split families and can divide churches (see I Corinthians 3:1–9). In the case of Cain and Abel, jealousy led to murder.

We must understand and accept that God made each of us unique. We each have different personalities, different likes and dislikes, different gifts and talents. Even with our differences, however, we were all created "in the image of God." We need to be thankful for who we are and be respectful of others.

In team sports, there is no such thing as a "one-man team." A team is only as good as its weakest member. A team supports and edifies one another. A team depends upon each other for survival. A team works together in order to play the game and win the victory.

Teamwork is essential in the game of football; it is also essential in the game of life. There is no room for jealousy.

Oh, Lord, help us to recognize any jealousy we may have in our own lives. Help us to acknowledge it as sin and bring it to you for forgiveness. Replace any jealousy with love for others and an understanding and gratefulness to you for the blessings you have given us. Help us to look at ourselves not with pride but with thankfulness. Let us not become jealous of others lest we destroy the very ones we love.

Questions to Ponder ...

- Why would Paul include jealousy in the "acts of the sinful nature" in Galatians 5:19–21?

- How do these acts contrast the "fruit of the Spirit" found in Galatians 5:22–23?

- How does Galatians 5:26 fit into the lesson of jealousy?

The Generations of Adam (Genesis 5)

This chapter is full of numbers. I work for university faculty who teach natural sciences, mathematics, and computer sciences. I read this chapter and immediately thought of our mathematics faculty. The writer of Genesis evidently thought it was very important that we not only know the names of the generations of Adam but that we also know their ages.

Have you ever noticed that the math adds up? We are told the father's age when the first son is born. We are told the number of years the father lived after the birth of his son. We are told that the father had other sons and daughters. Finally, we are told the father's age when he died. In each case, the numbers add up to the total stated. These people lived anywhere from 365 to 969 years of age! The writer of Genesis is quite detailed in his summary of the lives of Adam's descendants thus far.

It is also interesting to note the differences in

these detailed accounts. The first difference is the closing comment used for almost every generation: "and he died." In every instance this is true except for one: Enoch. Two very important details about Enoch are shared with us: "Enoch walked with God" (verses 22 and 24) and "God took him away" (verse 24).

The other difference is the additional information we are given about Adam and Noah. We are told that Adam had a son "in his own likeness, in his own image" (the image of God). We are reminded that man was created in the image of God. We are also told that the name Noah should comfort us in "labor and toil."

This chapter deals with the importance of life. The ages of these men were important. However, even more important than the length of life was the quality of life. Adam was created in the image of God, Enoch walked with God, and Noah would prove a comfort to man through his obedience to God.

The Lesson of the Importance of Life

We all are born, we all live, and we will all die (unless the Lord returns before that day and takes believers away to be with him). Let us look at each day as a gift from God. Let us look for opportunities to share happiness with others, to lessen burdens people may be carrying, and to bless others as we have been blessed. Let us share a smile and a greeting. May we be people who reflect God.

Oh, Lord, help us to recognize that life is important; it is a gift from you. Help us to live it daily to your glory, for we know not when this precious gift of life will end. When all is said and done, may it be said of us that we reflected your image, we walked with you, and we comforted others.

Questions to Ponder ...

- If this lesson is about the importance of life, what is the significance of the words "and he died"?

- Do you know of a person who died at an old age? Do you know of a person who died as a child? What do you remember about each?

- What did Jesus mean about having "life to the full" (John 10:10)?

Lesson 6: The Lesson of Preservation

The Flood (Genesis 6)

> The Lord was grieved that he had made man on the earth, and his heart was filled with pain.
>
> Genesis 6:6

What a terrible verse to read about God. The Sovereign Lord who created man is now filled with pain and grief caused by the wickedness of the very creatures he created for love and fellowship with him!

At the time of the flood, the Scripture tells us that "every inclination of the thoughts of [man's] heart was only evil all the time" (verse 5). How far we had fallen from our perfect presence with God in the Garden! Because of this wickedness, God decides to destroy mankind. "But Noah found favor in the eyes of the Lord ... Noah was a righteous man, blameless among the people of his time, and he walked with God" (verses 8 and 9).

Here is a perfect example of the lesson of preservation. God preserved Noah and his family because Noah knew and practiced the lessons of sovereignty and presence. Noah was obedient to God; therefore, he would not suffer punishment but would be preserved! But preservation was costly for Noah; he faced much ridicule for his obedience to God in building the ark. I am sure that Noah must have questioned in his mind many times this plan he was carrying out at the Lord's command, but his obedience preserved not only him and his family but also the entire world.

The Lesson of Preservation

When we are going through trials in our lives, it is sometimes difficult to sense God's presence, much less his preservation. Sometimes what may be God's preservation seems more like God's punishment. There are times when we stand up for something or someone, and it feels like we are standing alone. There are times when our standing for what is true and right brings ridicule and pain—even what may seem to us as betrayal or desertion by God.

It is times like these when we need to remember that God is sovereign, he is still in control, and he will bring us through the trial. Even though "the Lord was grieved...and his heart was filled with pain," he still chose to preserve the righteous, in this case, Noah. God will continue to preserve the righteous in times of trouble as he preserved Noah and his family through the flood.

Oh, Lord, thank you for the knowledge that you preserve your people. Forgive us when we are so overcome by trials that we cannot see your hand of preservation. We know you honor obedience and bless faithfulness. Thank you for your love and care.

Questions to Ponder ...

- What trials have you been through in which you sensed God's preservation?

- Have you faced ridicule, criticism, or slander because of your stand for God and/or righteousness? After standing, in what ways did you discover God's preservation?

- Do we always see God's hand of preservation when we are going through trials?

Lesson 7: The Lesson of Obedience

The Ark and the Flood (Genesis 6 and 7)

I must linger at the story of Noah and the ark, for there are many lessons for us to learn in this historical account: lessons of obedience, faith, trust, hope, worship, praise, and thanksgiving. Many are the illustrations of these lessons in the Scriptures, but this one event contains them all. In the account of the flood, we see God's sovereignty, his presence, his punishment, yet his preservation—all because of one man's obedience.

If Noah had not obeyed God, the world and everything and everyone in it would have been destroyed. Because of obedience, the earth was saved and given a "rebirth," so to speak. Mankind was given a second chance, and God himself made a covenant with mankind and sealed it with a mark that we still see today: the rainbow.

God loves obedience. God loves us and does not want any of us to perish, to die without knowing him in a personal, close relationship.

God was present with Noah throughout the flood,

loving him, guiding him, teaching him, saving him, using his creation to show Noah the power and pre-serving hand of the sovereign Lord God Almighty.

The Lesson of Obedience

> Does the LORD delight in burnt offerings and sacrifices as much as in obeying the voice of the LORD? To obey is better than sacrifice, and to heed is better than the fat of rams.
>
> 1 Samuel 15:22

God loves obedience.

> And this is love: that we walk in obedience to his commands. As you have heard from the beginning, his command is that you walk in love.
>
> II John :6

We are to walk in obedience to the Lord's commands.

These Scriptures are representative of the commands we are given in the Word to obey the Lord. Obedience is paramount to the Lord. Obedience, however, is sometimes difficult.

As parents we expect obedience from our children. If they disobey, they suffer the consequences of punishment. As citizens, we are expected to obey the laws of the land. If we disobey, we suffer the consequences of punishments of fines, trials, imprisonment, and/or death.

As human beings we are to obey the Lord. He provided a way for our salvation through the sacrifice of his one and only son, Jesus Christ. It is God's will that all be saved, but we have the freedom to make that choice. If we choose the Messiah, Jesus Christ, we choose eternal life. If we refuse, we choose the ultimate punishment, eternal damnation.

To choose obedience is to choose life.

Oh, Lord, help us to recognize your voice and obey your commands. Help us to demonstrate this obedience to our families, that they, too, will learn to obey your commands.

Questions to Ponder ...

- What do you think about when you see a rainbow?
- Have you ever been given a "second chance"?
- Why is obedience so difficult sometimes?

The Landing of the Ark (Genesis 8)

> But God remembered Noah and all the wild animals and the livestock that were with him in the ark...
>
> Genesis 8:1

Isn't it wonderful to know that God remembers us! What a wonderful lesson for us to learn. God "remembered" Noah. God provided for Noah. God took care of Noah. God brought Noah to land, to safety, to peace, to a new home.

God used his creation of the dove to bring word to Noah. The dove brought back the olive leaf, not only a symbol of new life on earth but also a symbol of peace on earth! No more evil. No more wickedness. No more anger and bitterness and fighting and wars—only peace and the promise of new life.

Isn't that the lesson of remembrance? Remember the thief on the cross at Christ's crucifixion who asked to be "remembered" when Jesus came into his kingdom (Luke 23:42)?

Oh, God, remember me! Remember me when I

struggle with temptation, with pain, with doubts, with fears. Remember me when it seems like life's problems are flooding over me. Remember me, and bring me peace.

The Lesson of Remembrance

Do you remember everything you did three days ago? What about three months ago? Do you remember your best friend when you were a child? Do you remember the first time you rode a bicycle? Do you remember your first steps? Do you remember your first words? God does.

God remembers us! He remembers seeing us growing and developing in our mother's womb. He remembers our first tears of sadness. He remembers our praises we sang last Sunday. He does not remember that lie we told last week, however, because we asked him to forgive us. God remembers us!

From this lesson we learn that when God remembers he also rescues and restores. He rescued Noah and his family and all the animals from the flood. He restored not only creation but also his relationship with mankind.

When we think about people we love, we remember how they look, how they act, their personalities, the fun times we have had with them, and the hard times they have been through. God is like that, too. He remembers us and the trials we are facing and going through. He hears our prayers and he remembers. He comes and sits with us once again and gives us peace.

Oh, Lord, thank you for remembering us. Thank you for remembering us when we celebrate the good times. Thank you for remembering us when times are rough and life is complicated. Please remind us that you remember.

Questions to Ponder...

- Do you think God needs reminders to remember?
- When was there a time when God remembered you and suddenly stepped into the scene and rescued or restored?

Lesson 9: The Lesson of Promises

God's Covenant (Genesis 8 and 9)

Promises! Promises! We make them all the time. Some we make to others; some we make to ourselves. Some we keep; some we do not. Some we wish we had never made; some we wish we had never broken. The promises of man are like sinking sand, but God's promises are firm and sure. God keeps his promises!

Here in Genesis, God makes some powerful promises.

> Never again will I curse the ground because of man, even though every inclination of his heart is evil from childhood.
>
> Genesis 8:21a

> Never again will I destroy all living creatures, as I have done.
>
> Genesis 8:21b

> As long as the earth endures, seedtime and harvest, cold and heat, summer and winter, day and night will never cease.
>
> Genesis 8:22

Never again will all life be cut off by the waters of a flood; never again will there be a flood to destroy the earth.

Genesis 9:11

God makes a covenant—a promise—with Noah and all mankind in the future, and then God creates a way to "remind himself" of his promise:

Whenever I bring clouds over the earth and the rainbow appears in the clouds, I will remember my covenant between me and you and all living creatures of every kind.

Genesis 9:14–15

The Lesson of Promises

Promises are important. May we not be so quick to promise something we cannot deliver. May we give careful prayer and thought to the promises we make.

Oh, Lord, help us not to make hasty promises when faced with guilt or problems. Help us to see promises as words of integrity and holy covenants. May the promises we make to our children be kept so that the lesson of promises be learned early in their lives.

Forgive us for breaking our promises to you. Even as you remind yourself of your promises when a rainbow appears, may we remind ourselves of our promises to you and to others.

Questions to Ponder ...

- What kind of promises do we make to others and to ourselves?

- What kind of promises do we make to God?

- What happens when we break our promises?

- What can we do to improve in this area of our lives?

Lesson 10: The Lesson of Heritage

The Lists of Names (Genesis 10)

So many times, we "skip over" the lists of names given in the Scriptures. You know the ones I mean—the *begats* and *begottens,* the sons of, the descendants of, the clans of, the generations of, the nations of, and on and on. I do not know if we do this because we are afraid we will pronounce a name wrong, show our ignorance, or just do not see the importance of reading all those names! But there is a lesson here to be learned: the lesson of heritage!

We all are descendants of Adam who was created by God. We all are members of one race: the human race. We all are members of humanity.

It is interesting to note that everything in the Bible is there for a reason. The Bible is not only a letter from God to us, but it is also a "lamp to my feet and a light for my path" (Psalm 119:105). It is to show us where we are now, help us move ahead in life a step at a time, and shine a light ahead of us. It shows us "the way" in darkness or when we do not know the way to go.

All those names are also in the Bible for a reason. They are people who lived, who obeyed the Lord or ignored him, who gave their lives for their faith or taught others the way, or who opposed the Lord and were punished accordingly.

They represent families, parents, children, rulers, peasants, the rich, the poor, the slave, the free, the Jew, the Gentile, the good, the bad, the sinner, the saint—you and me.

They faced problems like we face. They made mistakes like we make. They had hope when hope seemed lost. They had faith in one they could not see or hear or touch. They believed stories that had been told to them from generation to generation. They remembered battles, victories, and losses. They knew times when God fought for them and when prayers were answered. They had skills and talents that they used in service to the Lord or they buried and hid from sight or allowed Satan to use. There were those who risked their lives for the sake of the Gospel.

They were people just like you and me.

The Lesson of Heritage

We, too, have a heritage—not only a biblical heritage but also a national heritage. We have ancestors who sacrificed so that we can be here today. We have a heritage of those who fought for our freedom from oppression—politically, physically, and spiritually. Freedom is costly.

Oh, Lord, help us to remember that everything in the Bible is there for a reason. Help us to look for your truth. Teach us, Lord, through these people. Thank you, Lord, for those who have fought for our freedoms. May we never take their sacrifices for granted. May we leave a Christian heritage for our descendants who follow us.

Questions to Ponder ...

- What are some stories you have been told about your heritage and your ancestors?

- What people in the Bible helped you when you were facing trials or unusual circumstances?

The Tower of Babel (Genesis 11:1–9)

Have you ever heard the phrase, "Pride goes … before a fall" (Proverbs 16:18)? It seems synonymous with the Tower of Babel.

Once again, mankind was all caught up in being so good and knowing so much that we wanted to be bigger and better and taller than anyone else.

Sound familiar? We have to have better homes than our neighbors, drive newer or more expensive cars, have better clothes, better jobs, better this, better that …

God came along to the people of Babel and stopped all this "better than" nonsense. He confused their language so they could not tell each other how much better they were than their neighbors. The building of the "bigger" tower was stopped.

The Lesson of Pride

The lesson of pride teaches us that we should not consider ourselves to be better than our neighbor. Jesus taught us that we are to love our neighbors as ourselves

(Matthew 19:19b, among several others). Paul taught us to not think more highly of ourselves than we should, to humble ourselves before the Lord (Romans 12:3, and several other references in the Scriptures to humble ourselves).

Oh, Lord, help us with this lesson of pride. Lord, we are proud of accomplishments, both ours and our children's. We may be proud of our churches, our communities, our friends, and our families. But Lord, please help us not to let that honoring-type of pride grow into the "Tower of Babel" pride.

Questions to Ponder ...

- What is the difference between the "honoring-type" of pride and the "Tower of Babel" pride mentioned in the author's prayer?

- When is pride good?

- How can we tell when we "cross the line" between the two?

Lesson 12: The Lesson of Mortality

From Shem to Abram (Genesis 11:10-32)

After our "intermission" of the Tower of Babel, the writer of Genesis gives us more detail on the sons of Shem, specifically the lineage of Abram. Once again, age is evidently an important factor for us to know. The numbers, this time, however, are much smaller than we previously saw in chapter 5; the ages of men after the flood are much less than the ages of men before the flood. Why?

Perhaps sin had an effect on mortality. It was man's sin that brought on the flood. It was man's sin that brought about God's judgment. It was man's sin that "grieved the Lord...and filled his heart with pain" (Genesis 6:6). It was man's pride that built the Tower of Babel and brought God's "stop" to the plan. Perhaps it was better for man not to live so long.

Whatever the reason, the people in this passage of Genesis lived from 600 to 148 years. This is quite a decrease in mortality.

There is another important passage here, though, that shows God's mercy. That is the account of Terah, the father of Abram, Nahor, and Haran (the father of Lot). Once again, the writer of Genesis gives us needed history and explanation. Evidently, this particular family is noteworthy. Terah takes his family—his son, grandson, and daughter-in-law—and moves from Ur of the Chaldeans to go to Canaan, but they settle at Haran. Why did they move? Did this man know the Lord? Was his son, Abram, a believer? Did Terah, like Noah, find "favor in the eyes of the Lord" (Genesis 6:8)? Why did they stop at Haran? Maybe it was in memory of his son, Haran. We do not know the answers to these questions, but we know that the family settled there and Terah died there.

The Lesson of Mortality

Yes, there are consequences for sin. Perhaps our decreased mortality is one of those consequences; perhaps not. But God is sovereign. He is merciful; he will guide us if we let him.

Oh, Lord, Terah must have followed your direction to leave Ur. He must have also followed your leading to settle in Haran instead of proceeding to Canaan. Lord, help us to follow your leading when you speak to us. Help us to realize that we will not live forever; our years on this earth will also be counted some day. What that number will be, we do not know. But we pray the rest of those years will be spent following you and your ways.

Questions to Ponder ...

- What might be some reasons for the changes in the mortality ages stated here and in Genesis 5?

- What issues affect mortality now?

- What correlations, if any, are there between biblical history and truth and life and mortality now?

Lesson 13: The Lesson of Trust

The Call of Abram (Genesis 12:1–9)

Abram, later Abraham, is one of the strong examples in the Bible of a man of faith. Abram, however, had learned the lesson of trust before applying the lesson of faith.

Abram trusted God; he had known the Lord for many years. His father and his father before him had known the Lord. Abram had experienced the Lord's blessings in his own family. He had a God-fearing heritage. Abram trusted the Lord, so when God told him to leave Haran, he left.

There was a relationship of trust built between God and Abram. When God spoke, Abram listened and obeyed. God promised to bless Abram, and Abram trusted God to keep his promise. The more Abram trusted God, the more his faith in God increased.

The Lesson of Trust

Trust is foundational to our faith. In life, it is sometimes difficult to trust people. Even our best friends let us down occasionally. It may not be because they want to do so; sometimes situations arise and friends fail. Very personal concerns are sometimes shared in confidence for prayer and support. We share because we trust the person to keep our concerns confidential; however, later on we hear the concerns discussed in a group at the office. A husband may trust his wife to have dinner ready when he gets home because he has a meeting that night. When he arrives home, however, dinner is not even started. Their son became ill at school, and mom had to leave to pick him up and take him to the doctor. The wife let the husband down. Does this mean he should no longer trust her? Of course not.

Trust is built on relationships. Trust is also built, fortunately and unfortunately, on previous experience. As human beings, we sometimes betray trust or lose trust. God, however, is divine. He can be trusted.

Like Abram, we, too, can trust God. He knows us. He created us; he knows all about us—our comings and goings, our dreams and desires, our strengths and our weaknesses. We can trust him to lead us in paths of righteousness. He will not ask us to do something that will harm us. As we trust him in the little things, our faith will grow so that we can trust him in the bigger things of life.

Oh, Lord, help us to trust you. Help us to remember that you are sovereign, you are present, you are faithful. May we trust you.

Questions to Ponder ...

- What is the difference between trust and faith?
- Where does one stop and the other begin?

Lesson 14: The Lesson of Fear

Abram Lies about Sarai (Genesis 12:10–20)

Have you ever been somewhere that scares you? Have you ever been around people you think might harm you? Have you ever lied to protect yourself or someone you loved? Abram evidently found himself in this situation when he went down to Egypt.

This account seems strange to us. Why would Abram tell people that his wife was his sister? Obviously, from this passage, Abram was doing this for his own good. He was afraid he would be killed. However, he evidently did not think about the position in which he was putting his wife! She was taken into Pharaoh's palace to become another man's wife, a member of the Pharaoh's harem. If the Lord had called Abram to follow him and had told Abram all those wonderful blessings in Genesis 12:2–3, why would Abram risk the life of his wife and the promise of God? Answer: Abram was afraid!

God, however, was not thrown off-guard by Abram's lies. The Lord was present with Sarai and protected her. She was the wife of Abram; she was to be a mother, the mother of the promised heir. "The Lord inflicted serious diseases on Pharaoh and his household because of Abram's wife Sarai" (verse 17). Even though Pharaoh was innocent and knew nothing of Abram's lie, he and his household were punished.

As we all know, the truth always comes out. Abram comes out on the good end, acquiring sheep, cattle, donkeys, camels, and servants. Sarai is given back to Abram, and they are sent on their way.

It seems unfair that even though Abram lied, he seems to be "blessed" in Egypt. It also seems unfair that Pharaoh is punished for his innocence. Some things in life cannot be explained. We often seem to see the "righteous" punished and the "wicked" go free. We see this happen in court cases; we see it happen when innocent people are injured or killed and the guilty person goes uncaught or unpunished. We see the good and the bad killed in natural disasters. We see innocent people killed by terrorists.

The Lesson of Fear

In many instances, we may be overcome by fear. Our fears may be of small things, or they may be of large things. They may be imaginary; they may be very real. Fear, however, is not from God. Second Timothy 1:7 says, "For God did not give us a spirit of timidity [fear] but a spirit of power, of love and of self-discipline." Jesus told us in John 14:1, "Do not let your hearts be troubled. Trust in God; trust also in me." He emphasized that again in John 14:27b, "Do not let your hearts be troubled and do not be afraid." When we are afraid, we need to remind ourselves of these verses. We need to call on the Lord for strength and courage.

Oh, Lord, when we are afraid, draw close to us. Remind us of your presence. Help us think clearly and make the right choices. Help us, Lord, to overcome our fears with faith. Help us to stay true and honest and to trust in you in all things.

Questions to Ponder . . .

- Have you ever found yourself in a situation where you lied because you were afraid? What were the results?

- If you had it to do over again, what would you change? Why?

Abram and Lot Separate (Genesis 13)

Abram and Lot stood at a crossroad in life. The land could not support both of them and all their flocks, herds, and possessions. There was quarreling and fighting in the family. Abram saw the need for them to go their separate ways. As head of the family, he gave Lot "first choice" of which way to go. There were the lush, well-watered plains for his sheep and cattle; there were the conveniences of the cities. He chose the best for himself and his family (or so he thought).

Abram was satisfied—no jealousy or hard feelings on his part. He had recognized the problem and had asked God for wisdom and direction on how to solve the problem. He trusted God to show him what to do.

Abram was the leader of the clan. The decision was made to separate the two families. Lot was given his choice. He made his decision and moved his family into the plains, close to Sodom and Gomorrah.

Abram took his family into Canaan, a rugged and mountainous terrain.

And what was God's response to Abram's decision? He gave Abram and his offspring all the lands he could see to the north, south, east, and west—quite a reward for taking "second-best"!

The Lesson of Decision-Making

When faced with decisions, the first thing we need to do is to seek counsel from God. What would Jesus do if he were in this situation? We need to identify and weigh the pros and cons of our choices.

When my husband and I were faced with a major decision once, we had a pastor advise us to pray until we were neutral as to the decision. Once in that place, God could open and shut doors and lead us in the direction he wanted us to take. We found this to be excellent advice. Praying until we are neutral, praying for God's will, praying that God will open and shut doors in our behalf—all of these are ways to seek God's counsel.

We may be like Abram; God may ask us to give the other person "first choice." It is then that we need to be willing to take "second best" knowing that may be God's "first choice" for us!

Oh, Lord, when faced with decisions, may we always seek your will first. May we be watchful and recognize your answer.

Questions to Ponder ...

- How do you make decisions?

- As instructed in Romans 12:2, how are we able to test and approve what God's will is for us?

- Do you think God has a permissive will and a perfect will for each of us? Explain.

Lesson 16: The Lesson of God's Care

Abram Rescues Lot (Genesis 14)

Remember the old Martin hymn? "God will take care of you, through all the day, o'er all the way. He will take care of you. God will take care of you."

Imagine being Lot. There you are all settled into a new home—life is going well—and all of a sudden war breaks out practically in your backyard!

This had to be quite a battle. The Scripture says there were five kings against four kings, plus all their armies. This was not a battle fought hiding behind trees or wearing camouflage. Battles in those days were fought by forming battle lines and marching into each other. Those people living in the "war zone" and their possessions were considered the spoils or rewards for the victor's taking. Lot and his family and possessions were part of those rewards!

But God—do you not love those words! But God took care of Lot. Sending Abram news of Lot's capture, God was well ahead of what was happening. Abram called on his allies and his trained men, and they all went in pursuit of Lot. Abram's forces defeated the kings and brought back Lot, his family, and his possessions, as well as other people.

God took care of Lot and Abram, and Abram honored God.

There is more to this lesson. Because of Abram's obedience, he received the blessing of God. Because of Abram's life, God received glory for this victory. Abram honored God by giving a tenth of everything to God's representative, Melchizedek. He honored God even more by referring to him as "Lord, God Most High" when he spoke of God to the king of Sodom—"Lord, God Most High." Remember that lesson of sovereignty? The Lord God Most High is in control. He is to be worshipped and praised. He is to receive the glory.

The Lesson of God's Care

There are so many attributes to God. He is sovereign, he is present, he is powerful. He created us, he knows us, he loves us. He wants the best for us. He cares about us.

Oh, Lord, help me to remember that it is you, the sovereign God Almighty, who takes care of me.

Questions to Ponder ...

- What are some of the names for God in the Scriptures?

- According to Exodus 3:14, God told Moses that his name was "I AM WHO I AM." Where are other places in Scripture where God identifies himself as "I AM ... "?

- After having answered question two above, how do you feel about the lesson that God cares?

God's Covenant with Abram (Genesis 15)

It is always interesting to me as to how God speaks to us. Sometimes he speaks through a vision, as he did here to Abram. Sometimes he speaks through the Bible, sometimes through thoughts we have as we read or pray, sometimes through music, sometimes through other people (pastors, teachers, friends, relatives, and strangers). He speaks to us through our minds and our senses. It makes no difference how he speaks. The important lesson to learn is that he does speak.

In this chapter of Genesis, God gives assurance to Abram that God is his "shield" and his "very great reward" (verse 1). Wow! God is our very great reward! There is reason to rejoice in that statement alone.

But Abram shares his anxiety with God. Abram is worried about not having an heir. He is about eighty-five years old and has no one to inherit his estate.

But God has an answer! He assures Abram that he shall have a son, his own flesh and blood. Even more, his descendants shall be as many as the stars in the sky, so many they cannot be counted.

Abram believes God about his son and his descendants but questions God about possession of the land promised him. Again, God gives the answer—this time through prophecy.

A prophecy is a divinely inspired prediction, instruction, or exhortation; a true prophecy always comes to pass. The Bible is full of prophecies, some given by God himself and some given through God's chosen prophets. Many of them deal with the Messiah, Jesus Christ, but this prophecy by God was about a time long before the Messiah's birth and years beyond Abram's life.

Prophecies can be about good times or bad times. This prophecy shared by God with Abram is about bad times to come. Abram's descendants will be strangers in a strange land; they will be slaves and will be mistreated for four hundred years. But God will free them from their bondage, will punish their oppressors, and will bring them back to the land of Canaan once again, thereby fulfilling his promise to Abram.

And God promises peace and old age to his friend, Abram.

The Lesson of Prophecy

In today's world we have heard of people who claim to be the Messiah. We have heard of people who have "foretold" the end of the world ... and have been wrong. A true prophecy is always fulfilled. The Old Testament is full of prophecies about the Messiah, many of which have been fulfilled. If we are to trust in God, we must believe in his Word. One of the greatest prophecies has not yet been fulfilled—Christ's return. We must be ready.

Oh, Lord, help us to recognize those prophecies already fulfilled. Help us to recognize your hand at work in the world and in our lives, even now as we pray this prayer. Your Word is truth; your prophecies shall be fulfilled. Help us to be aware of false prophets, those who claim to be you or who claim to speak for you. Help us to hold fast to you and your teachings as we await the return of the King, the Messiah, the Lord, Jesus Christ!

Questions to Ponder…

- What are some prophecies in the Scriptures? Identify some given by God himself as well as some given by God's prophets.

- If they have already come to pass, how were they fulfilled?

Lesson 18: The Lesson of "Helping God"

Hagar and Ishmael (Genesis 16)

Have you ever tried to second-guess the Lord? Have you ever tried to help him out with a problem you have? If we are all honest, the answer to these questions is yes.

How many times have we prayed to the Lord, asking him to solve a problem, intervene in a situation, or perform a miracle … then we try to help him out! In our human nature, it is hard to give something to God to take care of and then step back and let him do it.

Surely Abram had shared God's promises to him with his wife, Sarai. Surely she knew that God had promised descendants to Abram; but being a loving wife, she, too, was worried about Abram having an heir. She was around seventy-five years old, and she had borne no children. Evidently, this promise was for Abram, not her. She would give her maidservant to Abram, and he would have a son by her.

Somehow, we try to help things come to pass when it comes to some of God's promises to us. And

CHERYL D. EDRIS

it seems like whenever we try to help God out along those lines, it always backfires on us.

So it was with Sarai and Hagar; neither was blessed by the other's attitude regarding this pregnancy.

But the Angel of the Lord found Hagar, and God once again makes promises. God's prophecy here is not one of great news, however. This man will be "a wild donkey of a man; his hand will be against everyone and everyone's hand against him, and he will live in hostility toward all his brothers" (verse 12).

God's words were true. Ishmael was all that God said he would be, and his descendants in Iraq and Iran continue the hostility. The arguments and wars between the descendants of Isaac and Ishmael have continued throughout all generations, even to the present—Israel and Pakistan, wars with Iraq and Iran, suicide bombers and terrorists.

But remember that first lesson? God is still in control! He was present with Hagar; he kept his promise to her—her descendants, also, are too numerous to count.

And what about Sarai, who tried to help out God with his promise to Abram? She, too, was blessed; for God is not only sovereign, he is also loving and forgiving.

The Lesson of "Helping God"

So many times we, as Christians, bring our concerns to the Lord in prayer. We know deep in our hearts that he is willing and able to answer these requests. Have you noticed, though, that it seems easier to believe for answers for others than it is to believe for answers for ourselves? We know God can heal so-and-so, but we are not quite sure he can heal us. We know he will provide for the neighbor down the street who just lost everything in a fire, but we are not sure he will provide the money for this month's house payment. Maybe we need to "help God out" with that one.

I remember a gentleman in the church I attended as a child. This man shared an illustration one time about prayer that I have always remembered. He said sometimes we are like the man who put his worries in a wagon and pulled it up to the altar. He prayed to God to take care of his requests, then promptly got up from the altar, picked up the handle, and pulled his wagon-load of worries back out the door with him.

This wise Christian man then shared that instead of being like the man with the wagon we need to be like the man with the dump truck. He, too, loaded up his worries and took them to the altar. There he also prayed to God to take care of his requests. He, however, got up from the altar, dumped out the truck, and went back home, leaving his worries at the altar for God to handle.

Yes, God may ask us to do our part in handling problems and trials in life; but we need not "help him" unless asked to do so. God is certainly capable of bringing his promises to pass.

Oh, Lord, help us to trust you and only "help" when you ask us to do so.

Questions to Ponder ...

- Have you ever tried to "help God"? What was the result?

- How hard is it to "dump our worries" at the foot of the cross and trust the Lord to take care of them for us? What do we need to do to trade in our wagons for dump trucks?

Lesson 19: The Lesson of Confirmation

The Covenant of Circumcision (Genesis 17)

Isn't God awesome! Once again, he confirms his promise to Abram; only this time is different. This time is God's time! Now, at age ninety-nine, Abram will see God's promise of an heir.

This is a new beginning for Abram; God makes it new by giving Abram a new name—Abraham—a name that has been remembered, revered, and respected throughout all generations to this present day—Abraham, the father of many nations. God reminds Abraham that his covenant is everlasting. He will be Abraham's God and the God of his descendants. The land of Canaan will be an everlasting possession.

There is a new covenant established here for Abraham as well: the covenant of circumcision. This time something is required of man; this is not a promise on God's part only. Abraham and his household must show their commitment to God. Circumcision is the sign of that commitment. Abraham and his descendants are to be set apart and known for their relationship with "God Almighty." They are to be God's "chosen people," the people who will receive the promises made by God to Abraham.

With God's confirmation of the birth of Isaac, the covenant of circumcision may also have been a sign of the marriage commitment between Abraham and Sarah. After these many years of marriage, God has confirmed his promise to them. He will bless them with a son. Years ago, "the two had become one flesh." Now their commitment to one another will be blessed with a child.

The Lesson of Confirmation

Perhaps God was trying to show man his value to God. Man was made in the "image of God," and man was the only part of creation that could pass along that "image" from generation to generation. God ordained the marriage relationship; he ordained the commitment required in that relationship, and he ordained that sex be a part of that commitment, a sacred and beautiful relationship between husband and wife within the bounds of matrimony.

This day in history marks time—time for new names for God's family, Abraham and Sarah; time for blessings to Abraham's sons, Ishmael and Isaac; time for sealing of a covenant with Abraham's promised son, Isaac, and all his descendants; and time for man to make a covenant with God.

And Abraham obeyed God and honored the covenant required of him. "On that very day," Abraham and every male in his household were circumcised.

Oh, Lord, may we always remember that you keep your promises and will confirm them with your people. May we, too, keep our promises and commitments to you.

Questions to Ponder ...

- Has God ever made a promise to you or asked you to do something and then later on confirmed it with you? Share those experiences and the impact they had on your life and your faith.

- What other times in Scripture do we see someone given a new name? What is the significance of this, from God's perspective? From the person's perspective?

The Three Visitors (Genesis 18)

The first lesson we need to learn from this passage of Scripture is the lesson of recognition. When God speaks to Abraham, he always recognizes God's voice. In this passage, God sends angels, and Abraham immediately recognizes these special visitors! Abraham quickly invites them into his home for food, drink, and rest. Abraham's whole household quickly responds to Abraham's instructions.

Again, we see God confirm the promise of Sarah's pregnancy, even though Sarah thinks this news is a joke.

The second lesson in this passage is the lesson of mercy. How many people do you know who would have the nerve to question God's plans so many times? Abraham must have had a very close relationship with God Almighty to have had the freedom to approach his presence and sovereignty and question his plans. What a fellowship! And what reverence and humility shown by Abraham toward the Lord God!

And what was God's reaction to Abraham's repeated questioning? His response was mercy. God knew Abraham's heart; he knew that Abraham was concerned about his nephew, Lot, and his family in Sodom. And God's answer of mercy showed Abraham that God would be true to his word and righteous in his judgment.

The Lessons of Recognition and Mercy

Hebrews 13:2 tells us, "Do not forget to entertain strangers, for by so doing some people have entertained angels without knowing it." Abraham immediately recognized his visitors as angels from God. This text in Hebrews refers back to this event.

It is important for us to remember that God loves us. He created us for fellowship with him. He loves to hear the praises and the prayers of his people. As we have already learned from previous lessons, God cares about us. He wants to communicate with us. He can do that in any way he sees fit—through trials, through people, through books, even through angels. The lesson for us to grasp here is the importance of recognizing God's voice. The only way we can do that is to spend time with him. Read his Word and talk to him. Just as we learn to recognize the voices of our parents or our children, so too, we can learn to recognize the voice of God.

Oh, Lord, may our relationship with you be so close that we always recognize your voice and your presence. May we show you reverence and humility, and may we recognize and appreciate the mercy you extend to us and our families.

_____

Questions to Ponder ...

- How do you recognize God's voice? How do you discern that the voice is truly God's?

- Have you ever "entertained angels unaware"? Does this still happen today?

- How would you define the word "mercy"?

Lesson 21: The Lessons of Protection and Judgment

Sodom and Gomorrah Destroyed (Genesis 19)

We see quite a contrast here between Abraham and Lot. Both men recognized the angels of God; both men treated them with respect, but the close relationship did not exist between Lot and God. Yes, Lot recognized the visitors as sent from God, but he did not readily obey their instructions. Even Lot's sons-in-law did not believe Lot when he told them of the Lord's plans. How did Lot know what the Lord was going to do? It makes a person wonder if Lot had mentioned the Lord to his sons-in-law before this night.

Lot hesitated when told to leave, so the men (angels) had to actually take hold of him and his wife and daughters and lead them out of town. Lot recognized God's favor, kindness, and mercy toward him; but his lack of faith showed when he requested to go to Zoar instead of the mountains as he was told.

Again...but God remembered Abraham's request and protected Lot from not only the evil men in the city but also from the total destruction of the city and the people living there.

But we need to see the other lesson in this passage: the lesson of judgment. Yes, God protected Lot, but God also carried out his judgment on the evil and wickedness of these two cities. God will punish sin; he will bring judgment. He is sovereign; he is in control. He is true to his word, and he will judge the living and the dead.

The Lessons of Protection and Judgment

Sometimes we get so caught up in the fact that God loves us that we miss the fact that he will also some day judge us.

> The Lord reigns forever; he has established his throne for judgment. He will judge the world in righteousness; he will govern the peoples with justice.
>
> Psalm 9:7–8

> For he has set a day when he will judge the world with justice by the man he has appointed.
>
> Acts 17:31a

> Then I saw a great white throne and him who was seated on it. Earth and sky fled from his presence, and there was no place for them. And I saw the dead, great and small, standing before the throne, and books were opened. Another book was opened, which is the book of life. The dead were judged

according to what they had done as recorded in the books. The sea gave up the dead that were in it, and death and Hades gave up the dead that were in them, and each person was judged according to what he had done. Then death and Hades were thrown into the lake of fire. The lake of fire is the second death. If anyone's name was not found written in the book of life, he was thrown into the lake of fire.

Revelation 20:11–15

Someday we shall all be judged. The only way we can have eternal life is to have our name written in the book of life. The only way that will happen is by accepting Jesus Christ as our Lord and Savior. Jesus said, "I am the way and the truth and the life. No one comes to the Father except through me" (John 14:6). We must confess our sins, repent and turn from our sinful ways, believe in Christ, and accept him as Lord of our life. Only by accepting Christ do we truly become God's child.

Oh, Lord, may we remember that you will protect your children, even from present and coming troubles and tribulation. But you will also judge the world, each of us. May our relationship be within "whispering distance" of our friend and our God. May we do what you tell us to do, knowing it is for our best and is according to your will.

[Note to Reader: If you have not accepted Christ as your Savior and you would like to know for sure that you are a child of God, pray the following prayer in sincerity right now: Lord, thank you for loving me. I confess that I have sinned and I am sorry for my sins. Please help me to turn away from them and follow you. Jesus, I believe that you died on the cross for my sins. I believe that you rose again and will some day return for your people. I now receive you as my personal Savior and the Lord of my life. Help me to trust in you and grow in my knowledge of and relationship with you. In your name I pray, Amen.]

Questions to Ponder ...

- Have you ever sensed God's protection in your life? What might have happened had he not been there?

- Does God have the right to judge the world and its people?

- When did you accept Jesus as your Savior? Share that experience with someone today.

Lot's Wife and the Pillar of Salt (Genesis 19:26)

There have probably been many sermons preached on this one event. Yet in this whole story of God's judgment on Sodom and Gomorrah and God's protection of Lot and his daughters, Lot's wife is only "featured" in this one verse.

In the story of Lot's settlement here in the plains of Sodom, we notice that he seems to be always moving closer to the evil of Sodom. First, he settled in the plains; then we find him at the city gates; then we find him in his home in the city. Then when protection and escape is at hand, Lot is reluctant to leave. Evidently, Lot's wife was also reluctant.

But are we not like that? When God tells us to move somewhere else or change jobs or careers or do something we have never done before, do we not tend to look back instead of following him and keep looking forward for his direction?

We do not know much about Lot's wife. We do

not know why she looked back. We do not know her thoughts, her motives, her heart; we only know that God's judgment was quick and final.

The Lesson of Looking Ahead

This is probably one of the hardest lessons for us to learn. Have you ever moved from a home you loved? You spent days going through everything you had accumulated since moving to this wonderful place you now call home. You reminisced over photos, cards, and gifts. It has been an emotional time of remembering. Finally, the day comes when you must leave. The truck is packed with all your belongings, the kids have told their friends goodbye, you have made one final walk through the house, and you get in your car. What is the last thing you do when you pull out of the driveway? You glance back for one final look at the home you are leaving.

What if someone told you to not look back? Maybe you need to catch a plane to go somewhere else. Maybe there is a blizzard heading your way and you need to leave quickly. What if it were God himself who told you not to look back? Would you listen?

When we want to move or we are anxious to move, we may not want to look back. We want to "shake the sand off our shoes" and move on. It is during those times, however, when we do not want to move that we will most likely look back.

This lesson, however, is not only about looking

back. It is also about obedience to God. Lot's wife was told not to look back, and she disobeyed.

We need to learn that there are times when God does not want us to look back. He does not want us to dwell on the past. He wants us to look to the future and trust him for something better. He wants us to forget the pain of past mistakes. He wants us to focus on him and the paths that are before us. In our obedience to him we will find joy and peace.

Oh, Lord, help us not to look back when you tell us to follow you. Help us to trust that you will lead us in the right ways. Help us to not be drawn closer to temptation and evil, but help us to draw nearer to you so that if you say go, we can do so without reluctance and without regret.

Questions to Ponder ...

- Have there been times when you have "looked back"? How did that affect your outlook toward the future?

- Have there been times when you did not look back? How did that affect your outlook toward the future?

Lesson 23: The Lesson of Influence

Lot and His Daughters (Genesis 19:30–38)

In this passage, we see the influence that the people of Sodom had on Lot and his daughters. We are not told how much time elapsed between verses 20 and 30, but it is interesting to note Lot's change of mind as to where he wanted to live.

In the previous passage, Lot just had to go to Zoar. There was no way he wanted to leave the plains, the cities, and go up into the mountains. He wanted to stay close to where he had been. After all, Zoar was a "very small" town. Surely that would be acceptable to the Lord.

Now all of a sudden we see in verse 30 that Lot was afraid to stay in Zoar. He took his daughters and gave up the city life to live in a cave!

Why would Lot change his mind? Did the life and morals (or lack thereof) in Sodom have this much influence on Lot? Did Lot think Zoar would be better than Sodom? Did Lot think Zoar would be similar to Sodom? Why was he afraid to stay in Zoar? Had the people heard what happened to Sodom and Gomorrah and somehow thought Lot and his family had something to do with the destruction of their neighboring cities? Were they threatening Lot and his family?

It appears as though the life in Sodom had more influence on Lot than Lot had on Zoar, so Lot chose to run to the mountains. Did he think God might destroy Zoar as well? Did he rethink his plans and decide to follow the Lord's original instructions? This passage brings many questions to mind but no answers.

There seems to be a lesson for us here, however: the lesson of influence. The sin of Sodom had influenced Lot and his family. It influenced his future sons-in-law, who thought he was joking about God (verse 14). It influenced Lot, causing him to hesitate, disobey, and bargain with God for a "plan B." And it evidently influenced Lot's daughters, as recorded in this passage.

Why would his daughters think of having sex with their father in order to produce heirs? Why not seek out godly men, marry them, and have families? It seems that would have been the natural thing to do, the right thing to do; but these girls had not seen the "right thing." They had lived in Sodom; that was the life they saw and knew. What a terrible influence the sins of Sodom had on these women. The older daughter even gave her son a name that meant "from father."

The Lesson of Influence

It has been said that we are judged by the company we keep. The behavior of Lot's daughters makes one tend to judge them as having been influenced by the people of Sodom. It was fine to practice incest and homosexuality there. Their father had even offered them to the men in the city when those visitors came (Genesis 19:8)! The most important thing to them was to give their father heirs, even if he were the father of his own grandchildren!

It has been said about influence that "you will either bring people up to your level, they will bring you down to their level, or you will split company." Lot's daughters had evidently been "brought down."

We are to have a positive influence on the people we meet. As Christians, we are to be examples of salt and light (Matthew 5:13–14). We are to "train a child in the way he should go, and when he is old he will not turn from it" (Proverbs 22:6). We are to live lives that reflect God and his teaching. In order to do these things, sometimes we have to make hard choices. We are to be testimonies to those we meet, but we are not to lose our children along the way.

As we make decisions, we need to consider the impact they will have on us, our families, our testimony to others, and our relationship with God. As we choose the company we keep, we need to keep in mind that we are to bring others to God and not be brought down to sin.

Oh, Lord, help us to realize the influence we have on others. Help us to realize that people do look to us for examples, guidance, and direction. Help us to point them to you. May we influence our children to follow your ways, your laws, your Word. May we be an influence that will bring glory and praise to you.

Questions to Ponder ...

- How do we walk that thin line of loving and sharing with others without becoming part of their lifestyles?
- How do we "hate the sin but love the sinner"?

Lesson 24: The Lesson of Responding to Truth

Abraham and Abimelech (Genesis 20)

Once again, Abraham lies about his relationship with Sarah, telling the people that Sarah was his sister. After everything that God had done for Abraham, one would think he would know better. On the other hand, do we not do the same thing sometimes?

Have you ever repeated the same mistake? Have you ever told the Lord that you will never do something again; then later on you do it? The Apostle Paul wrote about this struggle with sin in Romans 7:14–15. Paul recognized that we do things we do not mean to do or do not want to do. The important lesson to learn is to recognize the truth that we have sinned and ask the Lord for his forgiveness.

This passage mentions Abraham's sin, but it focuses on Abimelech and his response to the truth—that Sarah is Abraham's wife, not his sister.

It is interesting to note that God is the one who revealed this truth to Abimelech, who immediately pleads innocent of any wrongdoing to Sarah. Abimelech asks God for mercy for him and his nation. He returns Sarah to Abraham and also gives livestock and slaves to Abraham as a token of his apology and desire to make things right. Abimelech also speaks to Sarah, telling her that he is giving silver to her "brother" in an effort to correct this mistake.

Abimelech's response to the truth showed his respect for the Lord and his concern for his people. We are not told how long Abraham and Sarah had been in Gerar, but it was long enough to notice that Abimelech's wives had not been able to conceive (verses 17–18).

Abimelech responded to the truth he was given. He took action and asked for mercy, and his household was healed.

The Lesson of Responding to Truth

As we mature both physically and spiritually, we are to learn from our mistakes. To confess our sins and repent does not mean to go ahead and repeat the same sin over and over again expecting God to continually forgive. Yes, God forgives our sins. Yes, we may make the same mistake again … and again. To repent, however, means we turn away from our sin; we do a complete u-turn and start to follow God's ways. We are not to intentionally continue to sin and expect God to pat us on the head and tell us that it is okay. Nor are we to try to tell God that is "just the way we are."

With God's help, we can change. The Apostle Paul tells us in II Corinthians 5:17, "Therefore if anyone is in Christ, he is a new creation; the old has gone, the new has come!" As soon as God reveals a truth to us, we need to act on it—confess our sin, ask forgiveness, and make it right. I John 1:9 tells us, "If we confess our sins, he is faithful and just and will forgive us our sins and purify us from all unrighteousness."

Oh, Lord, help us realize that when you reveal your truth to us, we need to respond. As your children, we have a responsibility to obey your truth. When you reveal a sin to us, help us to recognize and confess that sin and ask for your forgiveness. Help us also to repent of that sin and not do it again.

Questions to Ponder ...

- Has God ever told you to go to someone and ask forgiveness from him or her? Did you do it? What was the result?

- Has God ever asked you to go to someone to resolve a conflict? Did you do it? What was the result?

- Do the above situations always "come out right"? Why or why not?

- What is the lesson to learn?

Lesson 25: The Lesson of Laughter

Isaac Is Born (Genesis 21:1–7)

Rejoice! A son is born to Abraham and Sarah! Even in their old age, God has blessed them with a son! "At the very time God had promised," Isaac was born! And Sarah said, "God has brought me laughter, and everyone who hears about this will laugh with me" (verse 6).

The wonderful gift of laughter—have you ever been so overcome with joy that you burst out laughing? Have you experienced those times when God's blessings to you have overflowed? Have you ever had those times when God has miraculously answered your prayers? Someone you love has been healed! Someone for whom you have prayed for years has been saved! A family who has suffered physical, emotional, and financial problems has now been blessed by God and they are rejoicing! Yes, we have experienced those times!

As I read this passage, I immediately thought of our son-in-law. When he and our daughter were expecting their second child, the doctors and ultrasounds all indicated that the baby was a girl. They labored over picking a name and had thought they would name the baby after a sister of each of them. We had all bought all those pretty little pink outfits and were ready to welcome this wonderful little girl into the family.

When the baby was born, my husband and I were the first to meet our new grandchild. Our daughter introduced us by saying something like, "Since the baby has been born, we decided to change the name. We thought Israel Micah might be more appropriate!"

You can imagine our reactions. "It's a boy! You have a son!" We were all ecstatic. When our son-in-law called his sister to tell her the news, he used a similar strategy, apologizing for not naming the baby after her but naming the baby Israel instead. I saw my son-in-law make that phone call (and several others). He was almost bent over with laughter and joy!

Romans 12:15 tells us to "Rejoice with those who rejoice; mourn with those who mourn." I imagine there were lots of people rejoicing with Abraham and Sarah that day! The Lord had fulfilled his promise; Isaac was born!

The Lesson of Laughter

I remember a pastor who once said that some Christians looked like they had been baptized in dill pickle juice! We need to smile! We need to laugh! We need to rejoice in the Lord for all he has done for us! Consider all the lessons we have seen thus far in the Book of Genesis. Think of all we have learned about God thus far, and we are not quite halfway through the book!

As you go through your day, take time to look around at God's creation. Notice the dewdrops on a rose. Listen to some of the songs of a cardinal. See how the trees glisten with frost. Watch the sailboats on the horizon. Watch the sunrise that awakens the earth and the sunset that lulls it to sleep. Listen to the children as they laugh and play. Hear the girls giggle as they talk to each other in a group. Stand in awe and pride as you hear the National Anthem and see the flag wave in the breeze. Laugh at yourself when you make a silly mistake. Give someone a hug and tell them you love them.

> Rejoice in the Lord always. I will say it again: Rejoice!
>
> Philippians 4:4

Oh, Lord, help us to rejoice with those who rejoice. Help us to burst into laughter at your unexpected blessings! Help us to recognize your grace in our lives and know that "at just the right time" you will fulfill your promises to us as your children. May we experience the gift of laughter, the joy of the Lord!

Questions to Ponder . . .

- Does it seem harder to "rejoice with those who rejoice" than it is to "mourn with those who mourn"? Why or why not?

- Have you ever been so overcome with joy that you burst out laughing? Share that experience with someone.

- Have you experienced those times when God's blessings to you have overflowed? Share those experiences with someone.

Lesson 26: The Lesson of Letting Go and Letting God

Hagar and Ishmael Sent Away (Genesis 21:8–21)

It's a party! Isaac has been weaned. He has grown from a baby to a small child, and there is a celebration!

However, not everyone was celebrating. Evidently, Ishmael was making fun of or "mocking" the festivities, and Sarah became upset. One can almost hear the disgust and disdain in Sarah's voice as she tells Abraham to, "Get rid of that slave woman and her son ... "

But Ishmael was Abraham's firstborn son. He was not the son of promise, but he was Abraham's son. Verse 11 tells us that "the matter distressed Abraham greatly because it concerned his son."

Here again, God assures Abraham that all will be fine; Ishmael will become a nation.

Thus, Abraham gives Hagar food and water and sends her on her way with Ishmael. Obeying God, Abraham let go and let God take care of his son, Ishmael. Indeed, the Scripture confirms that "God was with the boy as he grew up" (verse 20).

The Lesson of Letting Go and Letting God

Letting go and letting God can be so hard sometimes. As parents, we reach that point where we need to let go of our children and trust God to take care of them. This is much easier when our children have their own faith in the Lord. It is much more difficult when they do not know the Lord. However, even in the best of circumstances, this lesson is hard to follow.

Someone once said, "Once a parent, always a parent." We try to do our best at raising our children. In my denomination, there is a question in the baptism or dedication of infants or children that is directed to the parents as follows:

> Do you promise with the help of God to bring him/her up in the nurture and discipline of the Lord, to pray with him/her and for him/her, and to make every effort to so order your own life that you will not cause this little one to stumble?

It is ideal to raise our children "in the nurture and discipline of the Lord"; but if we do not have that relationship with God, we cannot share that blessing with our children. No matter what our age, however, when we ourselves accept the Lord, God can help us share that experience with our children. Perhaps one of the greatest lessons we can teach them is to "let go and let God." Allow your children the blessing of seeing that lesson in your life.

Oh, Lord, help us with this lesson. Help us to raise our children so that they can stand on their own and will trust and obey you. If they can do this, it will be much easier to "let go." Lord, too, help us to let go of our worries, our problems, the unknown, those things that can bog us down in our walk with you. Help us to "let go and let you" take care of our lives. You know our future. Help us to trust you with it.

Questions to Ponder ...

- If you were raised in a Christian home, how did your parents "let go and let God"?

- What are some obstacles you have faced when "letting go and letting God"?

- Do you know someone whose children have rebelled against God and their parents? How are the parents handling this situation? What could you do to help?

Treaty at Beersheba (Genesis 21:22–34)

Once again, Abimelech enters the picture. He has been good to Abraham. His people have treated Abraham well. Now Abimelech and the commander of his forces come to see Abraham about a matter of national security. Abimelech's opening statement says it all: "God is with you in everything you do" (verse 22). What a testimony Abraham has been to Abimelech! God's presence with Abraham is obvious even to unbelievers! Then Abimelech makes a request of Abraham. He asks Abraham to swear an oath that Abraham will not deal falsely with Abimelech, his children, or his descendants. He goes on to ask that Abraham show the same kindness to Abimelech and his country that they have shown Abraham. Abraham agrees.

When one thinks about it, these two requests were quite literal and pointed. Abraham had lied to Abimelech in the past (Genesis 20). That deceitfulness had an effect on Abimelech's people and country. Abimelech does not want this deceitfulness repeated!

Also, Abimelech had shown kindness to Abraham. He had given Abraham sheep, cattle, slaves, and money—and he had allowed Abraham to settle wherever he wanted. Abimelech now asks that Abraham treat him and his people with the same kindness, reminding Abraham that he is an alien in Abimelech's country.

This time, Abraham gives the sheep and cattle as a token of his agreement. The matter of the well dug by Abraham is also settled by Abraham, giving the additional seven lambs. The two men made an agreement; they swore an oath to each other, and the contract was signed and sealed by the giving of property and a king's word.

"And Abraham stayed in the land of the Philistines for a long time" (verse 34).

Abimelech was a good king. He recognized the strengths of one who would be a good ally. He was proactive with the terms and conditions of the treaty. He had been true to his word in the past and would be true to it in the future. He basically asked Abraham to do unto him that which Abimelech had done unto Abraham.

The Lesson of Making Agreements

In the past an oath was your bond. A handshake between two people used to be considered a binding agreement. Now, we have to have pages of legal contracts, signed by all parties involved, to constitute an agreement. Somewhere along the way, our word became worthless.

When teaching about oaths, Jesus told us in Matthew 5:37, "Simply let your 'Yes' be 'Yes,' and your 'No,' 'No'; anything beyond this comes from the evil one." Jesus also taught us that we are to "do to others as you would have them do to you" (Luke 6:31). We are to treat people in the same way we want to be treated.

We need to revive the trust that our word used to give. We need to practice standing behind our "Yes" and our "No." We need to make agreements that we mean and keep them.

Oh, Lord, that we as people and nations would honor these principles today—respect for each other, trust in each other, using our word as our bond, treating each other as we wish to be treated. Abimelech was the king; he set the example for his people. Oh Lord, help us to set a trustworthy, respectful example to others. Help us to be honest when making agreements. Help us to abide by them. Help the nations of the world to also follow these principles. May the "leaders" of countries be *leaders* of their countries. May they follow Abimelech's example in this passage of Scripture. May they make lasting treaties that will give honor to you.

Questions to Ponder ...

- Why has "a handshake and a promise" become void?

- Have you ever had an agreement with someone based on an oath? Was the agreement kept? If so, why do you think that happened?

- How can we practice and improve our "Yes" and "No" answers?

Abraham Tested (Genesis 22)

When I hear or read this story, I am amazed, amazed at the lesson of faithfulness that is presented here. This faithfulness, however, is two-person: God and Abraham.

We are told right at the very beginning that God tested Abraham; God was testing Abraham's faithfulness. Notice how God tells Abraham to take his son, his only son whom he loves, and sacrifice him as a burnt offering. Can you imagine God telling you to sacrifice your one and only son as a burnt offering? God must have had a lot of faith in Abraham's obedience.

And Abraham must have had a lot of faith in God's promises. God had promised to bless Abraham with many descendants; and that blessing was to be through Isaac. Abraham trusted God—even with his one and only son. Abraham's relationship with God was so strong that his obedience was based on faith in a promise.

Abraham trusted God completely. He told his servants that he and Isaac would worship, and then both would come back to them. Abraham told Isaac that God himself would provide the lamb for the offering.

His obedience was again rewarded by God's faithfulness and blessing. Once again, God is faithful and "provides"—not only the sacrifice but also a recommitment to his covenant with Abraham. This time God swears by himself to make Abraham's descendants as numerous as the stars in the sky and the sand on the seashore. God goes even further, telling Abraham that all nations on earth will be blessed through his offspring.

The Lesson of Faithfulness

Abraham was faithful to God by trusting him, even in a tremendously tough time of testing. Abraham trusted God to provide. Abraham believed God and his promises, and he trusted God to keep his promises.

Sometimes we think faithfulness is a one-way street—only God has to be faithful to us; we do not have to be faithful to him. At other times, we may think faithfulness is the other way around. In this lesson, however, we see that faithfulness is a two-way street. God is faithful to us, and we need to be faithful to him.

God was faithful to Abraham, not only on that day but forever. God provided the sacrifice for Abraham that day; he saved Abraham's one and only son. Hundreds of years later, God showed his faithfulness to his promise by sending his one and only son whom he loved, Jesus Christ, as a sacrifice for the sins of the whole world. All nations on earth have been blessed through Abraham's offspring, Jesus Christ.

Oh, Lord, help us to trust your faithfulness, your promises, your plans. May we prove faithful to you in our times of testing. May we also trust you to "provide."

Questions to Ponder ...

- Was there ever a time in your life that God asked you to do something you did not want to do? Did you do it?

- What was your attitude toward God when obeying (or not obeying) his command?

- What was the result?

Lesson 29: The Lesson of Integrity

The Death of Sarah (Genesis 23)

Once again, we see the character of Abraham. He has just lost his wife, Sarah, whom he loved all these years, the wife of his youth, and the mother of Isaac, to whom God's promise was given. We see Abraham as he mourns.

It is not a lesson in mourning, however, that I notice. It is the evidence of Abraham's integrity. He is obviously highly respected in the community. He is referred to as "a mighty prince among us" (verse 6). It seems he could have had anything he wanted, but Abraham approaches his neighbors with humility, saying that he is "an alien and a stranger among [them]" (verse 4). He requests that he be able to buy property so that he can bury Sarah.

Most likely, any of the men there would have been willing to give Abraham the land, but Abraham wanted to make sure that everything was done properly and legally. He did not want to leave room for rumor, gossip, or accusation. He was a man of integrity and sought the people's help and the rightful purchase of the property he wanted. He paid the price quoted by the owner; all was done in the presence of witnesses. Abraham respected Ephron, and Ephron respected Abraham. There was no cheating, bickering, bartering, or haggling during the negotiation. The worth was named, the price was paid, and the land was deeded to Abraham. His integrity was apparent to all.

The Lesson of Integrity

Abraham was a man of his word. He was well known in the community. People had heard his words and observed his actions for years. "The walk and the talk" matched! He was a man of integrity.

We, too, need to be people of integrity. Learning and applying the commands and lessons of God will help us to achieve that goal. It is a life-long lesson. Integrity is built over time through many experiences. Applying the Lesson of Agreements will help to establish the Lesson of Integrity.

Oh, Lord, may we always seek to be respectful of others and treat them the way we want to be treated. May our yes be yes and our no be no. May we be known as people of integrity that we may bring honor and glory to you.

Questions to Ponder ...

- How do we build integrity?
- How does someone exhibit integrity?
- Why is integrity important?

Isaac and Rebekah (Genesis 24)

Even on the verge of death, Abraham's faithfulness in God holds firm. He calls on his chief servant, the one in charge of all that he had. Abraham tells the servant directly what to do and how he should trust God to guide and lead him. Abraham tells his servant that God will even send an angel before him. Abraham gives specific direction to his servant, and his servant swears an oath to carry out the instruction.

This man obviously respected Abraham—and his God. We see that the servant had learned the importance of prayer, asking God for success and kindness to his master, Abraham.

The servant wants to make sure he follows God's will and chooses the right woman for Isaac, so he prays to the Lord for some specific direction. This girl will be friendly, will offer him a drink of water, and will even offer to water his camels. And before he had finished praying, there was Rebekah, a beautiful young woman who did everything the servant expected.

Abraham had been right about his God; he was

faithful. He did hear prayer and grant petitions. He did send his angels before this servant and prepared Rebekah and her family. And he led this servant directly to them!

What a lesson of testimony! God did exactly what Abraham had said he would do—and God did it for the servant as well as for Abraham! So what did the servant do? He testified to Rebekah's family about all that God had done to bring him to them!

The Lesson of Testimony

One tells one, who tells one, who tells another one—and on it goes.

There is no stronger evidence for God's existence and love than the personal testimony of a believer. How can we share about something we have never experienced? How can you tell someone how something tastes without having them taste it?

One does not have to share his or her faith in a certain way. We do not have a script to follow or a stage on which to speak. God is personal to each of us. He speaks to us in different ways. He leads us according to our needs. To share one's testimony is simply to tell someone else what God has done for you!

Those who hear may be going through similar circumstances. They may be going through similar trials. If God helped you and has made such a difference in your life, maybe, just maybe, God can change their lives, too.

When God prompts you to testify to someone about him, do so. Share from your heart. Ask God to give you the words to say. He will do so; and you, too, will become a witness for God.

Oh, Lord, help us to testify to the things you have done for us. May others see your love and faithfulness not only to us but also to them as they trust in you.

Questions to Ponder ...

- Do you have a testimony of what God has done for you? Share it with others.

- How do we lead someone to the Lord? What do we say in order to help someone accept Jesus as his or her Savior?

- [Note to Reader: If you have never shared your faith and want to learn more of how to do so, talk to your pastor or to someone you know who has shared his or her faith with you.]

The Death of Abraham (Genesis 25:1–18)

The story of Abraham's life comes to an end. Even in his final days, he was conscious of his fatherly responsibilities and his love for his children.

Here we learn that Abraham had married after Sarah died. Keturah had borne him six sons.

> Abraham left everything he owned to Isaac. But while he was still living, he gave gifts to the sons of his concubines and sent them away from his son Isaac to the land of the east.
>
> Genesis 25:5–6

Abraham loved his sons, and he wanted the best for them. The promises and blessings of God, however, were to go through Isaac. "The torch" was to be passed to him.

We are left with a wonderful eulogy of Abraham in verse 8: "Then Abraham breathed his last and died at a good old age, an old man and full of years … " His sons, Isaac and Ishmael, buried him with his beloved Sarah in the cave near Mamre in the field decded to him by the Hittites.

Ishmael's sons are also listed in this passage. Abraham loved Ishmael, and God had also made him into a nation as he had promised Abraham. Ishmael's sons became tribal rulers in their settlements and camps. Some of these names sound familiar even today. We are left, however, with a sad epitaph in verse 18b: "And they lived in hostility toward all their brothers."

There is quite a difference here between the descriptions of Abraham and that of Ishmael's descendants.

What else can be said of Abraham? He lived his life, he followed the Lord, and he "passed the torch" to his son, Isaac. "After Abraham's death, God blessed his son Isaac ... " (verse 11).

The Lesson of Passing the Torch

It is important to us as we age that we have someone to whom to "pass the torch." In most cases, this is a torch of leadership in a family that is passed to a son or daughter. We may, however, be passing a torch of leadership in a business or a ministry. It is important that we "pass the torch" to someone who shares our beliefs and our morals. Again, we need to be testimonies and examples to others of our faith in God and our desire to follow his will and direction in our lives. May our "torch" light the way for others to follow.

Oh, Lord, help us, as parents, to pass the torch of faith to our children. May we live as examples of your truth and grace. May we, as your people, share your love with others that they too may be saved. May our "lights" so shine before men that they may praise you (Matthew 5:16).

Questions to Ponder ...

- When God calls us to other ministries, businesses, places of leadership, how difficult is it to "pass the torch"?
- If we have a choice, how do we determine to whom we "pass the torch"?
- When we are forced to "pass the torch," how do we reconcile ourselves to the task?

Jacob and Esau (Genesis 25:19–34)

The whole story of Jacob and Esau, the twin sons of Isaac, covers several chapters in Genesis. It is a good story to read all the way through and then look back to see what lessons can be learned. Their lives contain many lessons for us.

The first lesson is that quick decisions may be costly.

In reading through the story (Genesis 25 through 33), it was interesting to note that God knew about Jacob and Esau even as they were in the womb. God told Rebekah that these would be two nations, two peoples separated, one stronger than the other, and the older would serve the younger (Genesis 25:23). When one looks at all the deceitfulness in this story, it all ended up being as God had said it would be.

This first lesson about quick decisions took place when Jacob wanted Esau to sell him his birthright for a bowl of stew. What was Esau thinking? Yes, he was hungry, but to give up his birthright as firstborn son for a little food? This birthright had to do with his inheritance, his family, leadership, and promises. Esau did not take time to think through this decision, to consider the cost of what he was doing—and this decision cost him greatly.

The Lesson of Costly Decisions

We make costly decisions all the time. Let's go here now, or buy this now, or make quick decisions about careers, choices, jobs, relationships—never stopping to consider what the cost may be later on. We want things now when sometimes we would be better off to wait until we had the means to afford what we want or had the knowledge to make a more informed decision.

We need to pause and consider the consequences that might occur because of our decisions. We need to pray and seek God's counsel. If we are facing a decision wherein the answer seems rushed, strange, or confusing, maybe we need to stop and rethink it. When we are so confused that we cannot seem to see a clear answer, perhaps the answer is not from God. Pray that God gives you a clear answer, one that, if followed, will not harm or destroy you.

Decisions can be costly. Ask for divine direction. Stop to consider the possible effects. Do not rush in.

Oh, Lord, please help us to pray more and seek your will instead of jumping to quick decisions. Help us to be content to wait until we can afford that which we want, for perhaps we may not want it as much as we first thought. As someone once said, "Sometimes when we get what we want, we get more than we bargained for." Help us to count the costs before we make a decision.

Questions to Ponder...

- Why is it sometimes so difficult to practice "delayed gratification" (postponing a purchase until we have the money)?

- In our fast-paced society of fast food, drive-up banks, pharmacies, and restaurants, how do we convince ourselves to slow down to count the costs when making decisions?

Isaac and Abimelech (Genesis 26)

Have you ever heard the phrase that "history repeats itself"? Well, Isaac and Abimelech are good examples. Reading this chapter is like rereading chapter 20.

Surely Abraham must have told the story to Isaac about how he lied to Abimelech about his wife, Sarah; how God came to Abimelech, found him innocent, and opened the wombs of the women in his household; and about the treaty made between Abraham and Abimelech. Did Isaac not learn from Abraham that lying about his wife was wrong? Did Isaac think this was the right way to deal with one's allies?

Notice the similarities between the two accounts. God had confirmed his promise to Abraham and Isaac. There was a famine in the land. Abraham and Isaac moved there. Both lied about their wives being their sisters because they were afraid for their own lives. Abimelech was an honorable man and, when finding out about the lies, gave orders to leave the women and their husbands alone. Abraham and Isaac were blessed. A treaty was made.

What is/are the lesson(s) in this chapter? I thought "hindsight was always 20/20." Why did Isaac make the same mistakes as Abraham?

Isaac seemed to go over the same steps that Abraham did in order to build his faith in God. He had to learn for himself that God would be faithful to him and would fulfill the promises he made to Abraham and to Isaac. Perhaps God was even confirming to Abimelech that he was God, the only true God.

Obviously, Abimelech saw the blessing of God upon Isaac, and that blessing worried him. Isaac had become powerful, and Abimelech was concerned for his own land and people. This time, Abimelech asked Isaac to leave; yet another treaty was made between the two men, and there was peace.

And Isaac's faith was built. He recognized God's promise, provision, and protection. Once again, an altar was built and a well was dug, and God received glory and worship.

The Lesson of Hindsight

Why do we make the same mistakes over and over again? Do we never use our "rear-view mirrors" to see what was done in the past? Sometimes I think that we live so much in the present that we forget to check out the past. In doing so, we might have a positive effect on our future. If we would take time once in a while to use hindsight, our current vision would be much clearer.

Why do we make the same mistakes as the people in the Bible? We make the same mistakes because we are human, and we have to have our own faith. We cannot make it on the faith of our parents, relatives, or friends. We have to have our own faith.

Some people think that because their parents or grandparents were Christians they, too, are Christians. We do not inherit Christianity; it is not part of our DNA or our genetics. Sin is what we have inherited; hell is our destination. Only accepting the Messiah, Jesus Christ, will alter our lives and our destiny. Philippians 2:12–13 tells us:

> Therefore, my dear friends, as you have always obeyed … continue to work out your salvation with fear and trembling, for it is God who works in you to will and to act according to his good purpose.

We need to spend time with God, getting to know him and his will for our lives. We need our own faith to sustain us.

Yes, we need to learn from history and from our mistakes so that we can make correct decisions now. Once a decision is made or something happens, "hindsight" will not correct it.

Oh, Lord, even when we make the same mistakes over and over again, you are there to forgive us and pick us up. May our faith in you grow as you show your faithfulness to us. May we remember and worship you. And may we not make the same mistakes again.

Questions to Ponder ...

- What are some things you have learned from hindsight?

- How can we apply these lessons to future decisions?

Jacob Gets Isaac's Blessing (Genesis 27:1–40)

And the friction continues between Jacob and Esau. Here we are in this "continuing saga" of the effects of deceit. Or is this deceit?

As one reads this account of Isaac's final blessing, one cannot help but wonder about Rebekah's instructions, motives, and behavior. We know from previous Scriptures that she knew even before her sons were born that they would be different, possibly quarrelsome, even that the older would serve the younger; for God himself had told her this (Genesis 25:23). We also know from Genesis 25:28 that "Isaac...loved Esau, but Rebekah loved Jacob." Further, we know that Esau married Hittite women, and "they were a source of grief to Isaac and Rebekah" (Genesis 26:34–35).

Whatever her reasons were, Rebekah is definitely behind this plan of deceiving Isaac for his final blessing. She is even willing to risk a curse (verse 13) in order for Jacob to receive this all-important blessing from his father, Isaac.

Jacob, however, goes along with this scheme. He has a chance to be honest with his father when Isaac asks who he is. But Jacob gives a full, detailed reply: "I am Esau your firstborn" (verse 19).

There is such painful emotion in this story of Isaac. He is old and blind and wants to make sure he gives his patriarchal blessing to his son, Esau. This is such an important and sacred responsibility—a once-in-a-lifetime experience. Although it appears that Isaac is skeptical that this son who comes is Esau, he believes and trusts him. Isaac richly blesses his son, only to find out shortly thereafter that he has been deceived and the blessing has been given to the younger son, Jacob.

Esau arrives on the scene, excited about pleasing his father and receiving the blessing. He, however, is devastated and pleads for a blessing from his father. Unfortunately, the only blessing Isaac can give to Esau is one of a hard life but eventual freedom from bondage.

What lesson does this account give us? What are we to learn? Was this deceitfulness? Yes. Was this a mother's love? Yes. Was this a son's true desire to please his father? Yes. Was this an example of God's sovereignty? Yes. God's plan was that the promise to Abraham was to go to Isaac and then to Jacob. Why? We do not know. Was it God's desire that it happen this way? We do not know. Knowing that God is sovereign, if it is in God's plan, he will bring it to pass—some way.

Was Rebekah "helping God" like Sarai tried? Was Rebekah pushing in where she did not belong? Or was she doing what God told her to do so that the blessing would go to Jacob? We do not know the answers to these questions, but we know there are always consequences to be paid for deceit. As this story continues, consequences follow.

But God is sovereign, and he is still in control.

The Lesson of Deceitfulness

This story is full of emotions and questions. Life is also that way. The Book of Genesis contains lessons we need to recognize, apply, or practice in life and lessons we need to recognize and avoid. Deceitfulness is one of those lessons we need to avoid.

There is nothing good about being deceitful. It causes pain and sorrow. It destroys our reputation and trust. It produces guilt and fear that the deceit will be discovered and punished. Our lives are too short to spend them "looking over our shoulder" in fear of reprisal.

Oh, Lord, help us to focus on you and your will. Help us not to judge, for we do not know all the answers. But, Lord, also help us not to deceive others but to be truthful, knowing that the truth will always come out.

Questions to Ponder ...

- Have you ever received something that was deserved by someone else? How did you feel?

- Have you ever expected an award or promotion but it was given to someone else instead? How did you feel?

- When deceit is involved, who is better off, the one who deceives or the one who is deceived?

Jacob Flees to Laban (Genesis 27:41–28:9)

Here, again, is another lesson present in this story. If we pick up the story where we left off, we find that Esau is angry with his brother, Jacob, and secretly plans to kill him. We see Rebekah's disgust with the Hittite women. We see Isaac's love for Jacob and recognition of God's plan that his promise is to go through the line of Jacob. We see Isaac knowingly blessing Jacob and commanding him to go to Paddan Aram to the house of his Uncle Laban to take a wife. We see Esau realizing how displeasing to his father his marriages to Canaanite women were. We see Esau trying to make amends with his parents by seeking a wife among Ishmael's family. (Esau was trying, but he went the wrong direction if he was trying to stay within the line of promise.)

Sometimes we need time to process things that happen to us. We need time to think, time to cry, time to be angry, and time to settle down, time to learn, time to understand, time … time … time.

The Lesson of Time

As we go through trials, time can be our friend or our enemy. When we are caught up in problems, we want time to pass quickly. We want our trials to be over. We want the storms and clouds to pass; we want sunshine and peace. When we are finally through the trial, we want time for quiet, peace, and healing.

We have no control over time; we cannot speed it up or slow it down. But it is a gift of God for us to use wisely.

Time—Yes, sometimes it does "heal wounds," but sometimes it just helps us to move ahead, one step at a time, to face a new day.

Thank you, Lord, for the gift of time.

Questions to Ponder...

- When you think about time, what do you think about?

- Why do you think God gives us time?

- How is time used in the Scriptures?

Jacob's Dream (Genesis 28:10–22)

God is so faithful, is he not? Here we see the Lord coming to Jacob to renew with him the promise given to Abraham and to Isaac. God wants Jacob to know that he is with Jacob and he will fulfill his promise.

Here we see the faith of his fathers become Jacob's faith. Jacob claims the promise as his own. He recognizes the fact that God is with him and will guide him.

Jacob is so excited; the Lord has spoken to him! "How awesome is this place! This is none other than the house of God; this is the gate of heaven" (verse 17). And Jacob called the place Bethel, the house of God.

The Lesson of Finding Bethel

Do you have a Bethel? Remember where you were when you first met God, when you asked him to forgive your sins and come into your life? That was your Bethel.

You know that quiet place where you can sit and read and pray and talk to God? That is your Bethel.

Maybe it is a room, a closet, a chair, a park, a tree, a church, a tabernacle—wherever it is, for you, it is your Bethel.

Oh, Lord, help us find our Bethel today and talk to us. Help us remember when we first met you, and help us remember the excitement we felt in knowing that you love us and will be with us. Oh, Lord, how awesome you are! Forgive us today and renew in us a right relationship with you. Thank you for the fact that we can talk to you anywhere at any time. But thank you, too, for the Bethel in our lives, that very special place where we meet with you.

Questions to Ponder...

- Do you have a Bethel? Where is it?
- Why is your Bethel special to you?

Lesson 37: The Lesson of God's Hand

Jacob's Marriage (Genesis 29:1–30)

Jacob continues his journey, knowing that God is present with him. And so he was! The Lord leads Jacob right to the woman he is to marry—and it is "love at first sight!" How excited Jacob must have been. He found his mother's family, he was gloriously welcomed, he found the woman of his dreams, and his wages would be her hand in marriage.

Laban, however, does not deal with Jacob and Rachel in the same manner as he did with Isaac and Rebekah. Laban willingly released Rebekah to Isaac's servant, but in this story, Laban is deceitful with Jacob and tricks him into marrying Leah before he can marry Rachel. I wonder why. Had Laban heard of Isaac's wealth and blessings? Did he see a good chance to get free work and also find a good husband for Leah? Obviously, Jacob must have been a good worker since it was a "whole month" (verse 14) that he had been there before Laban offered him wages for his work. Was this deceitfulness of Laban's a sort of consequences for Jacob's deceitfulness with Isaac or was this God's hand moving in the midst of deceitfulness to turn it for good?

We see many times in the Bible—and in our own lives—where God intervenes and uses man's or Satan's schemes for his glory. God can turn what Satan means for harm to something God uses for our good! And it seems like a lot of that is based on our reaction to "the bad" that comes our way.

Yes, Jacob was upset by Laban's trick! Jacob went to bed with whom he thought was his beautiful Rebekah, but he woke up to find himself married to her sister, Leah. But Jacob did as Laban said. He stayed with Leah, and he worked another seven years for Rebekah. And God turned something meant for harm to a multiple blessing for good.

The Lesson of God's Hand

This lesson is an important one for us to learn. Even though God is sovereign and he remembers us and can turn bad to good, there are still consequences to pay for our sins and our mistakes. Laban learns this lesson as well, as we follow this story on through the Scriptures.

The more we grow in the Lord, the more Satan tries to stop us. As young Christians, Satan tries to tell us that we are not saved, we have been too bad to be saved, God cannot and will not forgive us, we cannot be a Christian, we will never make it, we should give up. These are all lies of the Devil. There is nothing that God cannot do, and "I can do everything through him who gives me strength" (Philippians 4:13).

Satan will try to throw things in our path to distract us from following God, but we need to trust God to bring us through. It is when we look back that we will see God's hand at work in our lives and situations.

Oh, Lord, help us to see your hand when something "bad" enters our lives. Help us to see you in the midst of the circumstance. Help us to stand firm and keep going, knowing that you are working everything out for our good. And when we get through the storm, help us to look back, recognize your hand, and testify to your love and presence in our lives.

Questions to Ponder ...

- When going through trials, how can we reach out for God's hand?

- How do we know he is really there when we cannot see him or feel him?

- How can we talk to him when we are so depressed or ill that we cannot even pray?

Jacob's Children (Genesis 29:31–30:24)

Can you believe the behavior of these women? Surely we do not behave like this now! Or do we?

I read this account and see women fighting over the love of one man, trying to make him love each of them more. Who can please him the most? "If I cannot give him children, then I will give him my maidservant and let her give him children." One can almost hear the bickering and the "I am better than you" or "My maidservant is better than your maidservant!" Where is the lesson here?

Stop the bickering!

First, God sees that Leah was not loved by Jacob, so God opens Leah's womb so she can conceive. She gives birth to four sons: Reuben, Simeon, Levi, and Judah—and she gives praise to the Lord.

Then we see Rachel become jealous and angry and accusatory toward Jacob. Her solution to the problem is giving Jacob her maidservant, Bilhah. Then Bilhah gives birth to two sons, whom Rachel names Dan and Naphtali.

Leah has to keep up, so she gives Jacob her maid-servant, Zilpah, who gives birth to two sons. Leah names them Gad and Asher.

And then we come to the ultimate deal where Rachel lets Leah sleep with Jacob in return for some of Reuben's mandrake plants (believed to have the power to induce conception). So Leah "hires" Jacob to sleep with her, and she conceives Issachar … and later Zebulun. A daughter, Dinah, is also born to Leah later on.

> God remembered Rachel; he listened to her and opened her womb. She became pregnant and gave birth to a son and said, "God has taken away my disgrace." She named him Joseph …
>
> Genesis 30:22–24

Once again, "God remembers." Just like God remembered Noah and his family and took action bringing about the flood, God remembered Rachel and opened her womb so that she could conceive, and God's promise was renewed through Joseph.

I wonder what Rachel said that prompted God to "listen to her." I wonder if she asked for God's forgiveness for her jealousy and anger, for the bickering and scheming between her and Leah. I wonder if she confessed her love for God, for her husband, and for her family. Whatever she said, "God listened."

The Lesson of One-Upmanship

Why do we think we have to be better than someone else? Why do we think we can manipulate God and life? Why do we think we need to "help God" bring about his promises to us? The answer is the same to these questions as to some of the previous ones in this study—we are human.

However, being human is not an excuse for disobedience to or lack of faith in God. Sometimes it helps for us to re-read Scripture and review lessons learned in order to remind ourselves that God is in control, he does hear and answer prayer, he does love us, and he does care.

Oh, Lord, help us to remember that you are in control. We need not try to stay "one up" on anyone—not our neighbor, not our family, no one. Yes, you blessed Jacob with eleven sons, and your promise continued; but your blessing surely was not because of two women bickering over one man's love. Help us remember that "you remember" and you are faithful.

Questions to Ponder...

- How did the culture of the day explain the marriage and children relationship shown in these verses?

- Do we try to get God's attention today by trying one-upmanship? If so, how?

Jacob Flees from Laban
(Genesis 30:25–31:55)

In this passage of Scripture, we see the completion of the time of Jacob working for Laban. Jacob has now been in Paddan Aram for twenty years. He worked for fourteen years for Leah and Rachel; he worked an additional six years for his flocks.

Jacob was obviously a good shepherd and a good businessman. His acquisition of his flocks by using the striped sticks during mating was not only a genetic theory but also an instruction from God through a dream. Even though Laban agreed to Jacob's wages, Laban again was deceitful in his dealings with Jacob. The very same day the agreement was made, Laban removed all the goats that could possibly give flocks to Jacob. However, God was with Jacob, and God blessed Jacob with large, strong flocks.

Laban had been deceitful with Jacob from the beginning, and he had taken advantage of Jacob for twenty years. But during those last six years, things began to change. Jacob was coming out on top—God was blessing him, and Laban's sons were not happy, and neither was Laban.

Then God spoke, and Jacob made plans to leave Paddan Aram, taking his children, his wives, all his livestock, and any other goods he had accumulated while he was there. Jacob left without telling Laban, and the deceit continued.

But with deceit usually comes consequences. This story is no exception. Laban took advantage of Jacob, and Jacob ended up with a family and strong flocks. Jacob was deceitful with Laban when he left without telling Laban. And as we recall, Jacob had been deceitful to his father, Isaac.

So how much of Jacob's life was "payback" for deceitfulness? And how much of Laban's life was also "payback" for his deceitfulness?

In the end, both men came together, an agreement was made, a "witness" was established, and God received the praise. Laban had the opportunity to kiss his daughters and grandchildren good-bye and bless them, and Jacob took his family and started home.

The Lesson of Consequences

Twenty years had passed for Jacob, twenty years of hard work away from home; but he was finally going home.

This is a hard lesson to learn. We think that because we change or we ask forgiveness that we will not have to suffer consequences for our actions. Unfortunately, this is not always true.

When our children do wrong, sometimes it seems like it was an innocent mistake. Their punishment for disobedience could be anything from a time out to a spanking to being grounded for a month. Age and circumstances dictate the type of consequences—but consequences are still part of the punishment. If a "small lie" is left unpunished, it can lead to a lifestyle of telling more and bigger lies, for the only way to cover a lie is to tell a bigger one. If you tell a big enough lie long enough, it can be seen as truth. Deceit has come full circle, lives are destroyed, and truth is buried in the chaos of deceit.

Let us be mindful of deceit. Let us teach our children the importance of telling the truth and the importance of seeking forgiveness when we sin.

Oh, Lord, help us to be truthful and honest in our dealings with others so that we do not have to experience the lesson of consequences.

Questions to Ponder ...

- Have you ever told a lie and then found you had to tell another and another to cover it up? What were the results?

- Have you ever been on the receiving end of deceit? Did you have others to help you through that time of trial? Were you able to forgive?

Jacob Prepares to Meet Esau (Genesis 32:1–21)

This passage is alive with events and emotions. Jacob is finally returning to his father after these many years. But Jacob appears to be a little concerned about his brother, Esau—and for good reasons. Jacob deceived Esau; Jacob took Esau's birthright and blessing. Jacob fled for his life as Esau was plotting revenge against him. What will this meeting bring? Will Esau welcome Jacob, his family, and his possessions with open arms or with open hostility? The thought of meeting four hundred men was a bit alarming!

Jacob, therefore, makes a plan; he prepares for his meeting with Esau. He divides those who were with him into two groups and selects gifts for his brother. He also gives instructions on what is to be said when the gifts are given. Jacob puts off his encounter with Esau, and the gifts go ahead of him, as do his family and possessions. Jacob, however, spends the night in camp.

Jacob needs time to prepare himself to meet Esau. It has been twenty years since Jacob has seen his brother, his twin brother. Someone has to make that first move to resolve broken relationships. In this case, Jacob is the one making that move.

Jacob tries to pacify his brother by sending gifts ahead. Jacob is preparing Esau for their meeting. Jacob emphasizes the instructions to his herdsmen to say, "Your servant Jacob is coming behind us" (verse 20). Jacob wants Esau to know that he is returning with a servant's heart; and even though he has acquired a great many possessions, he deeply desires to heal the rift between himself and Esau. They are brothers; they are twin brothers. Surely, deep within their souls, there is love, respect, and brotherhood.

Yes, Jacob prepares. He prepares his family. He prepares his herdsmen. He prepares Esau. Now he needs to prepare himself. Thus, Jacob stays behind, by himself, to ponder and prepare for whatever is to come the next day.

The Lesson of Preparedness

Perhaps you know of siblings who have been separated for years and then see each other again. Perhaps you know of families who have been split for years by anger, jealousy, bitterness, or misunderstandings. When they see each other again, it could make matters worse. It could, however, usher in forgiveness and reconciliation.

It was God's intent that families be one, that they love and respect each other, that the bond among them be close. When that bond between people is broken, however, someone needs to make the first move to restore the relationship. That takes preparedness.

Sometimes we have to prepare ourselves. We need to be willing to forgive and to be forgiven. We need to want reconciliation to occur. We need to humble ourselves. We need to think through what needs to be done and what needs to be said. We need a plan of action.

Beyond long-term breaks in relationships, each day holds challenges of its own for us to face. We need to prepare ourselves daily for those challenges. We need to be "prayed up" for whatever may come our way.

Oh, Lord, are we prepared today for whatever may come our way? Help us to plan ahead. Help us to seek your ideas, your mind, your direction. Help us to rest in you and let you prepare us for whatever lies ahead.

Questions to Ponder ...

- How can we prepare ourselves for that which each day will offer?

- Is the giving of a gift to someone when asking forgiveness trying to "buy" their forgiveness or showing that we are sorry and wish to be forgiven?

Lesson 41: The Lesson of Encountering

Jacob Wrestles with God (Genesis 32:22–31)

Here we find Jacob alone, "and a man wrestled with him till daybreak" (Genesis 32:24).

Do you ever wrestle with decisions, thoughts, habits? I had to "wrestle" with this chapter of Scripture to find the lessons for me.

Before Jacob encountered his brother, he had to encounter God. He needed to face God; he needed to encounter God personally, face-to-face. Jacob wrestled with God as with a man. Man could not win, but God did. Thus, Jacob knew that God was in control and was watching over him and his family.

Yet Jacob asked for God's blessing! God's presence was not enough; Jacob needed God's blessing. Jacob had stolen a blessing once before: the blessing from his father, Isaac. This time Jacob *asked* and he *received*—freely, abundantly, faithfully. Jacob was given a new name. No longer was he Jacob, the deceiver; now he was Israel, one who struggles with God. His new name would remind him of this encounter with God, of his human weakness, of God's mercy in sparing his life, and of God's blessing on his life.

The Lesson of Encountering

Sometimes we wrestle with our faith; we want to know why something happened. We want to know why we have to go through trials. Sometimes we feel that God has deserted us or betrayed us. It is during these times that our faith is built or lost.

Sometimes trials leave us with hurts, or consequences, or other kinds of reminders. Hopefully, wrestling with our faith and seeking out God's truth will help us to see that he is still in control, he still loves us, his hand is still working, and he will bless us if we will let him.

It does not matter how long we have been a Christian, we can still wrestle with our faith. We are not perfect; we are emotional beings who need to know that God is present. We need the confirmation that everything will work out for our good.

No matter what or who we have to encounter each day, we need to first encounter God and ask for his blessing on our lives.

Oh, Lord, we need you today. We need to know you are here. We need to encounter you before we encounter anyone or anything else. Fill us with your Spirit; fill us with your blessings. Give us direction this day.

Questions to Ponder ...

- Have you "wrestled" with God in the past? What was the outcome?

- Have you encountered problems when you were glad you had encountered God earlier? Were you better prepared to handle the situation than you would have been on your own?

Jacob Meets Esau (Genesis 33)

Has God ever asked you to go to someone and ask his or her forgiveness? If so, you can understand a little how Jacob must have felt as he went to meet Esau. It had been twenty years since they had seen each other, twenty years since they had spoken. At that time, Esau wanted to kill Jacob because of his deceitfulness regarding Isaac's blessing; and now Esau is accompanied by four hundred men.

Jacob humbly approaches, bowing down timidly. Esau, however, runs to meet and welcome his brother. Evidently, Esau has forgiven Jacob and has longed to see his brother. Esau questions Jacob as to all these people, flocks, herds, and camels, all these that were sent ahead by Jacob to Esau. He tells Jacob that God has also blessed him. He welcomes his brother and family and offers to accompany them the rest of the way home. When Jacob refuses the offer, Esau suggests some of his men stay with the group, but Jacob refuses.

Esau welcomes a brother; Jacob returns as a servant. Esau heads back home, and Jacob settles where he is.

This passage shows a brother who has already forgiven and forgotten the past, one who himself has been forgiven and blessed by God, one who is thrilled to see his brother at last, and one who wants to join together again and live in peace. The other brother is unsure, skeptical, and hesitant. His experience over the last twenty years has probably contributed to this reaction. He feels he has to pay for his brother's forgiveness and acceptance. He insists that his brother take all that is offered, and he also makes sure there is still some distance between them.

God, indeed, had gone before Jacob. God had prepared the way. God had blessed Esau just as he had blessed Jacob. God had kept his word. God had softened Esau's heart, and God had mended a broken family.

Should Jacob have been more trusting of his brother, Esau? Should he have trusted God more and gone with Esau? These are questions for which we may never have answers. The lesson here is that God does go before us; he does prepare the way, and we can depend on him to do the same for us when we approach someone to ask for forgiveness. We need to be forgiven; we need peace of mind; we need restoration; we need each other; and we need God.

Israel (Jacob) acknowledged that he needed God's

presence, God's provision, and God's answer. Once again, he built an altar; but this time it was the God of "Israel" whose name was praised. God had given Jacob a new name, a new start, and a new family. Israel sealed his gratefulness to God.

The Lesson That God Goes Before

Sometimes it is very scary to go to someone and ask forgiveness. We do not know if we will be welcomed or whipped. We do not know if the person will listen or lash out. We pray that God will go before us to prepare the way, but we may still fear that we are on our own and subject to the other person's moods and feelings.

This is when we need to have faith in God and trust him. We need to reach out in love knowing we are doing what is right and trusting that God will work it all out for his glory.

Oh, Lord, please continue to go before us, preparing the way, especially when times are tough and we are unsure of the outcome. Help us to know that you are there and that you will answer. You are our God; help us to always praise you.

Questions to Ponder ...

- Have you ever felt compelled to go to someone and ask forgiveness? Did you find that he/she was upset with you or that he/she did not even realize there was a problem?

- Were you ever worried about a situation and then arrived to find that there was no problem at all? Had God gone before?

Dinah and the Shechemites (Genesis 34)
Jacob Returns to Bethel (Genesis 35)

This passage gives us a shot of reality, a look at culture, law, and religion at that time.

Jacob's daughter, Dinah, goes out to meet and visit the women of the land there. Shechem, the son of the ruler of the land, however, sees Dinah, wants her, takes her, rapes her, and keeps her in his house. Then Shechem tells his father to get Dinah as his wife. He wants her, but nowhere in the Scripture do we see that Dinah has any romantic feelings for her rapist.

Jacob and his sons hear of this despicable sin done to Dinah, and they are furious. Shechem's offer to pay anything, do anything, give anything they want for Dinah's hand in marriage probably did not impress them, but it did give them a plan for retaliation. They request that all the men in the city be circumcised. When Shechem and Hamor relay this request to the men at the city gate, we see the hearts of the ruler and his son. Circumcision is a small price to pay for the acquisition of Jacob's family, flocks, and property. The agreement is made, legally binding at the city gates.

Three days later, Jacob's sons avenge the sin to their sister; they kill all the men, take all the women and children, plunder the city, and rescue Dinah. Jacob fears the effect this may have on him and his family.

Once again, God speaks and tells Jacob to go back to Bethel and build an altar to God. In turn, Jacob tells all who were with him to get rid of the foreign gods they had, to purify themselves, change their clothes, and go with him back to Bethel, back to the place where he met God.

The people do as they are told, and the foreign gods and earrings are buried under the oak at Shechem. "And the terror of God fell upon the towns all around them so that no one pursued them" (Genesis 35:5). They arrive at Bethel, and Jacob builds an altar to God.

It is interesting to note in this passage that Jacob is the name used, not Israel. When God comes, however, the name Israel is restored, and God blesses Israel once again.

The whole group moves on, but Rachel, Israel's beloved wife, dies giving birth to Benjamin. She is buried, and the family returns to the home of Isaac. Israel (Jacob) has now come full circle, back to his home, back to his father ... and Isaac dies. The Scriptures do not give us details about how long Israel was home before his father died, but it must have been a wonderful blessing for Isaac to see his son, Jacob, and his family after so many years.

"And his sons Esau and Jacob buried him" (Genesis 35:29).

The order of birthright was reestablished by the Word in Genesis 35:29: "Esau and Jacob buried him." The sons were home. Relationship was restored. Israel brought his family back to Bethel, back to God, and he brought them back to Mamre, back to his father and home. Isaac saw his sons reconciled and together, and he saw them each blessed by God. What better blessing could he receive before he died? Everyone was home—home with God, and home with each other.

The Lesson of Home

To me, there is nothing better than home. To most people home means family, love, laughter, safety, and peace. Unfortunately, to others home may mean quarreling, missing parents, strife, confusion, hatred, and fear.

God will help us establish his kind of home for our family. It does not matter the kind of home in which we were raised. If we ask him, God will help us establish a home that is under his leadership.

Oh, Lord, help us to have good memories of home. Help us have good relationships with our families. Help us to seek reconciliation with them when there are problems. May we be "at home" with them and "at home" with you. May we remember our "Bethel" and come home to you.

Questions to Ponder ...

- What are your memories of home? How has God helped you?

- Is the concept of having a heavenly Father something that is easy or difficult for you to accept? How has God shown you "a father's love"?

Esau's Descendants (Genesis 36)

This chapter seems to come out of nowhere and is an interlude in the story of Israel. For many chapters, we have been talking about Jacob, his life, his encounters with God, his return home. Now the writer of Genesis turns toward Esau. The writer gives us one chapter to introduce us to Esau's family. We are given one chapter about the brother who did not follow God's ways. However, it is very important, historically, that we have this chapter.

We first learn that Esau married women of Canaan. We learned earlier in Scripture that he had second thoughts and married a daughter of Ishmael as well.

We see that God had blessed Esau even though Esau did not love God nor did he follow God's commands. God blessed Esau even though his promises of great blessings were with Jacob. God is still over all.

Esau had five sons and many possessions, so many

that the land there could not support both Jacob and Esau's families because of their livestock. Because of this, Esau moved his whole family to a land some distance away from Jacob.

Now we meet Esau's family. This genealogy is different, though, from the others in Scripture. This list is repeated in three different ways.

First, we meet the wives and sons of Esau. Indeed, this was a large family.

Second, the writer of Genesis gives us a list of the sons and grandsons of Esau, his descendants called the Edomites, who lived in the country of Seir. This is important historical information. This tells us the name of the land and the name of the people: Edomites. It is interesting to note that Esau's name was also changed, or at least recognized as Edom instead of Esau.

Third, we are given the genealogy again, showing Esau's descendants as chiefs in the nation of Edom.

Then we are introduced to the other people living in the region as well as the rulers of Edom before any Israelite king lived.

Why so many names? Why duplicate lists? Why Horite genealogy?

The lesson here may be the importance of recognition. The Israelites and we today need to recognize that God is still over all that exists, even if his existence and sovereignty is denied. We need to recognize that this chapter provides history and gives evidence and support to the truth of Scripture.

"There, but for the grace of God, go I." We need to recognize that the history of these godless people could have been the history of the Israelites had they not followed God.

The Lesson of the Importance of Recognition

Sometimes we need to stop and think as to where we would be if not for God. We need to stop and "count our blessings." We are not to be arrogant or prideful or have a "holier than thou" attitude; we need to be humble and thankful to God for the differences he has made in our lives.

Oh, Lord, may we always recognize you in our lives. Help us recognize that, but for your grace, things that happen to others may have happened to us. Our lives would have been so much different without you, Lord. Help us recognize that you are still in control of the world, of nations, of people, of lives, of circumstances. You are "one God and Father of all who is over all and through all and in all" (Ephesians 4:6).

Questions to Ponder . . .

- What was your life like before you met God?

- What has your life been like since accepting Christ?

- If you had the chance, what would you have changed?

Lesson 45: The Lesson That God Is in Control

The Dreamer Is Sold (Genesis 37)

This chapter takes us back to Jacob, living in the land of Canaan, and then says, "This is the account of Jacob. Joseph ... " We had a chapter about Esau; now let's get back to Jacob and his descendants: Joseph.

We know Jacob (Israel) had twelve sons, but to talk about Jacob's descendants, the writer of Genesis starts with Joseph, the first son of Jacob's beloved wife, Rachel. Here we learn that Joseph is now seventeen years of age and is Israel's favorite son because Jacob was old when Joseph was born. Israel probably had more time to spend with Joseph than he had when the other boys were growing up. Israel may have had more time to talk to Joseph, to teach Joseph, to get to know Joseph. Israel loved Joseph so much that he gave him a beautiful fancy robe, one with bright colors that would stand out, one that probably should not be worn while working in the fields. This was a special gift for a special son. The result was jealousy and hatred among the brothers.

Can you not hear his brothers yelling at Joseph, talking behind his back, hurling insults at him, questioning their father's sanity? "What is father thinking? We are out here every day working hard to keep this family going. It's our sweat and blood being poured out here, and we don't get any special gift. We have worked all these years and not even received a young goat as a gift!" Somehow, this whole scenario made me think of the parable of the Prodigal Son that Jesus, the Messiah, told to his followers many years later (Luke 15:28–30).

If things were not bad enough, Joseph had a dream, a dream about his brothers bowing down to him. *'Absurd! How dare you think you will rule over us!'* "And they hated him all the more ... " (verse 8).

Then Joseph had another dream. One would think Joseph would have learned his lesson and not told his family about another dream, but no. He tells them all about the second dream. In this dream, not only do his brothers bow down to him but also his father and mother. That was too much for the brothers—but note the end of verse 11: "but his father kept the matter in mind."

That extra time Israel had to spend with Joseph may have given him more insight into Joseph and more understanding of his remarks. Israel knew Joseph well. Perhaps Joseph had dreams before, dreams that came true. Perhaps Israel knew that Joseph could interpret dreams. Perhaps Israel wondered if Joseph's dreams would be part of the family's future.

We do not know the reason that Israel "kept the matter in mind," but we do hear the planning and scheming of Joseph's brothers in retaliation to Joseph and his dreams. They see him in the distance coming their way, and they plot to kill him.

However, one brother, Reuben, thinks of a way to spare Joseph, to save him from death. He suggests that the brothers not kill Joseph but throw him in a cistern, a plan to which they agree.

I cannot help but think that Reuben breathed a sigh of relief, thinking he had saved Joseph's life and could take him back to their father, Israel. But no. While Reuben was evidently gone, Judah had a better idea. Upon seeing a caravan of Ishmaelites (is that not ironic), Judah suggests to his brothers that they not kill Joseph but rather sell him to these merchants. The deed is done; the transaction is made. The dream is destroyed, the dreamer is gone, the once beautiful precious robe is now stained with blood, and the brothers return to their father with their tale of Joseph's death. And Jacob mourned and "refused to be comforted" (verse 35).

Meanwhile, Joseph is sold in Egypt to Potiphar, the captain of Pharaoh's guard.

The Lesson That God Is in Control

This story is such a tragedy! Brothers sell their own brother, their own flesh and blood. These people claim to worship God, yet they behave in such a wicked way.

We read this story and think that this cannot possibly be right.

However, remember our first lesson in this series: the lesson of God's sovereignty? Here it is again. God is still in control. The Lord gave a dream to Joseph and a second dream as well. Joseph needs to keep his faith and trust in the Lord to get him through this terrible time.

We, as readers of this text, cannot see "the rest of the story" from our current perspective. We have not read on in the story to find out what happens. However, we do know that God is in control. He has made promises in the past, and he has fulfilled them to this point. We have no reason to mistrust him now.

When we are going through trials, through times that "cannot possibly be right," we need to remember this lesson. We need to hold onto this truth. We need to etch this lesson on our mind—God is in control! He has helped us before; he will help us again. He has not left us or forsaken us. He has promised to be with us. God is sovereign—he is in control.

Oh, Lord, help us to hold on to that truth when it seems like our whole world has caved in. Help us to have faith and trust in you when we cannot see you or feel you present. Help us when we feel like we have been thrown into a hole, sold to the devil, or are completely in darkness. Help us remember that you are in control. There is a light of hope, and you will lead us on and bring us to that place where you can use us best. Oh, Father, help us to know that you are in control and you will take care of us. Amen.

Questions to Ponder ...

- After Joseph was gone and presumably dead, did Israel remember Joseph's dreams? How do you suppose he explained the dreams and Joseph's "death"?

- Did Joseph's brothers think of his dreams or did they dismiss them after Joseph, the dreamer, was no longer around?

Judah and Tamar (Genesis 38)

Although the practices described in this chapter may seem strange to us, they were the law at the time. The writer of Genesis evidently wanted us to know some details about Judah, and yet we are not given all information. The Scripture tells us that Judah left his brothers; however, we are not told why. Maybe he had second thoughts about what he and his brothers did to Joseph; perhaps he wanted to be on his own. Whatever the reason, Judah left his father and brothers and married.

The Lord blessed Judah's marriage with children. Judah's first son, Er, however was wicked, so wicked that the Lord himself put him to death. This left Tamar, Er's wife, as a widow without children. As we read in this passage, Judah's second son was also wicked and was put to death by the Lord. No wonder Judah was hesitant for his third and only remaining son to sleep with Tamar, his daughter-in-law.

As the story progresses, though, it is quite evident that the Lord wanted his will and rules followed. The

Lord is just, and he expects us to do justly to him and to his instructions. Judah, himself, admits that he was wrong and Tamar was more righteous than he in following the Lord's commands. The tables are turned on Judah, and he sees the hand of God in the circumstances and outcome.

Judah does not sleep with Tamar again; he remains true to the Lord, and the promise of God continues through Judah's descendants. Tamar is also remembered by the Lord, not only by the blessing of having two sons, but also by the recognition given her in the "genealogy of Jesus Christ the son of David, the son of Abraham" in Matthew 1:1–3a.

The Lesson to Do Justly

The lesson to do justly illustrated by a woman who slept with her brothers-in-law seems like an oxymoron to us. This type of behavior in our society would, most likely, be questioned at the least.

The "do justly," however, refers to Judah's actions, not Tamar's.

We need to do justly with everyone we meet. We are not to put people in categories or judge them by their appearance or their actions. We are to share God's teachings and God's mercy with everyone.

We need to remember what the Lord requires of us: "To act justly and to love mercy and to walk humbly with your God" (Micah 6:8).

Oh, Lord, help us to follow your commands and

leading. Help us to deal with our families and others in a just and honest manner. Help us to stay true to you. Help us to remember what the Lord requires of us: "To act justly and to love mercy and to walk humbly with [our] God."

Questions to Ponder ...

- What does it mean to "act justly"?
- What does it mean to "love mercy"?
- What does it mean to "walk humbly with your God"?
- What is the significance of Tamar being mentioned in the genealogy of Christ?

The Dreamer Is Imprisoned (Genesis 39)

The Lord was with Joseph and he prospered…When his master saw that the Lord was with him and that the Lord gave him success in everything he did, Joseph found favor in his eyes and became his attendant. Potiphar put him in charge of his household, and he entrusted to his care everything he owned.

Genesis 39:2–4

From the very beginning of this chapter, we see that God is in control. The Lord is watching over Joseph; the Lord is blessing Joseph; the Lord is blessing Potiphar because of Joseph. The blessings of God are a direct result of the faithfulness of Joseph. This "well-built and handsome" young man was true to his faith and loyal to his master.

As in our lives, a time of testing came to Joseph. Potiphar's wife repeatedly tries to seduce him to go to bed with her. Joseph refuses to do "such a wicked thing and sin against God" (verse 9).

The scenario sounds like a present-day soap opera or, even more, like present-day life. It appears that Potiphar's wife has everything she has ever wanted—except this handsome Israelite, this Hebrew. When she is finally alone in the house, she grabs him by his cloak, knowing this time she will succeed. Joseph, however, has no intention whatsoever of giving in to this temptation. He runs from the house, leaving his cloak in her hand. Potiphar's wife, outraged at her seduction failure, lies to her husband about Joseph; and Potiphar "burns with anger" (verse 19).

Joseph could have been executed for this crime, but Potiphar puts Joseph in prison, "where the king's prisoners were confined." Joseph could have been thrown into any prison in Egypt, but Potiphar shows him grace. Evidently, the king's prisoners were kept under a type of house arrest while waiting for their sentencing. Why did Potiphar choose this prison for Joseph? Perhaps Potiphar knew his wife was lying about Joseph. Perhaps he feared Joseph's God or that he would lose the "blessing of the Lord" on everything he had (verse 5). Perhaps Potiphar did Joseph a favor because he liked Joseph and trusted him. On the other hand, perhaps God used Potiphar to accomplish his plan for Joseph's family. For whatever reason, Joseph is imprisoned with the king's prisoners.

Even though imprisoned, Joseph remains faithful to God; and God remains faithful to Joseph. The Lord continues to show kindness to Joseph; and, once again, Joseph is placed in a leadership position. This time he is in charge of all those in prison, and the Lord continues to give him success in whatever he does.

The Lesson of Faithfulness to God

No matter what, we are to remain faithful to God. We are to say and do whatever is right, even if we face ridicule, imprisonment, or even death. We must remain faithful to God. We have heard of teens who remained true to God but were murdered. We have heard of missionaries who remained faithful to God but were brutally killed by the very people to whom they ministered. We have heard of people who spoke their mind and stood up for their beliefs even though it cost them success and recognition. Being faithful to God can be costly, but that cost is nothing compared to the promise of eternal life given by God to his followers.

Oh, Lord, may we remain faithful to you, even in the worst of circumstances. May we stand for what is right and be examples for our children to follow, knowing that your love and the respect of our family are worth it. Like Joseph, may we remember that you have a plan for our lives and you will bring it to pass.

Questions to Ponder ...

- Do you know of people who were persecuted in some way for their faithfulness to God? Consider the circumstances and identify how God was faithful to them.

- Do you know of people who gave up something in order to follow God? What did they give up? What did they gain?

- Do you know of people who lost their position because of their beliefs but gained the respect of their family and others?

Lesson 48: The Lesson of Waiting

The Dreamer Is Remembered
(Genesis 40:1–41:13)

"Some time later," how long, we do not know; but "some time later" God intervenes once again in Joseph's life. This time it is through two servants of the King, a cup-bearer and a baker. Evidently, Joseph was a man who cared about others, who noticed their feelings and tried to meet their needs. These two prisoners were assigned to Joseph, "and he attended them."

"After they had been in custody for some time," they each had a dream the same night—two different men, two different dreams, two different concerns, but one need. They were worried, and they needed someone to interpret their dreams. Joseph noticed right away that something was wrong, and he asked them why they were so sad. The problem was there was no one there to interpret their dreams.

What was Joseph's answer? It was a simple solution: interpretations belong to God. Knowing that God would reveal to Joseph the meaning of the dreams, Joseph asks each of them to tell him the dream. Joseph then gives God's interpretation to both men. And both interpretations come to pass!

There is one other important element in this conversation and interpretation. Joseph tells the cupbearer:

> But when all goes well with you, remember me and show me kindness; mention me to Pharaoh and get me out of this prison ... The chief cupbearer, however, did not remember Joseph; he forgot him.
>
> Genesis 40:14, 23

The Scripture goes on to tell us that two full years passed before Pharaoh had the two dreams about the cows and grain. Joseph had been waiting all this time for the cupbearer to remember him. Two more years in prison; two more years even though he had done nothing wrong. Waiting, waiting, waiting. Waiting for men, waiting for God, waiting for answers ... waiting.

But then the chief cupbearer was "reminded of his shortcomings" (41:9), and he remembered Joseph. He told Pharaoh of this young Hebrew who interpreted their dreams, and whose interpretations came to pass. And Joseph was summoned to come before Pharaoh.

The Lesson of Waiting

Time seems to go so slowly when we are waiting for answers. A couple who has tried for years to have a baby waits one more time to find out the results of a pregnancy test. Will it be positive this time? A man just had a biopsy and he is waiting for the result. Will it be benign or malignant? A child is seriously injured in a car accident caused by a drunk driver. Will she ever walk again or will she be paralyzed for life? An aged mother has prayed all of her life for her son to be saved. Will she see her prayers granted before she dies?

Joseph was thrown into a cistern and sold by his brothers. He was imprisoned even though he was innocent. He was forgotten by the very person he helped. Do you suppose he ever felt like giving up?

When we are waiting for answers, it is tempting to not only lose our faith in God but also lose our faith in our fellow man. We are tempted to give up on both.

It is then that we need to remember Lesson One once again—God is sovereign. He will take care of us.

Oh, Lord, help us to not give up when we are waiting—waiting for answers that never seem to come, waiting for people to change but not seeing change take place, waiting for who knows what. Sometimes we wait and do not know for what or why we wait. Oh, Lord, help us to remember that Joseph waited, too; but he was remembered. You were still in control of his life. Maybe he needed to grow or change, or maybe the circumstances in Egypt needed to change. We do not know the reason for the "wait," but we know you did! Help us to remember that you know our reasons to wait, too!

_____

Questions to Ponder ...

- Do you suppose Joseph ever became angry because the cupbearer did not mention him?

- Do you suppose Joseph continued to care for those under his watch?

- What, do you suppose, kept Joseph going?

- Why do people continue to trust in God for answers to prayers that have been prayed for years?

Lesson 49: The Lesson of Leadership

The Dreamer Is Rewarded (Genesis 41:14–57)

Are leaders born or are they made? Some leaders have been members of families who are leaders. They have seen leadership modeled in their homes. Other leaders have learned from life experiences, observation, and training on how to become good leaders. How does one gain leadership? Some people think leaders "take over" or "assume" leadership. Others are "assigned" to leadership positions, and still others "earn" their leadership positions by being leaders.

Pharaoh summons Joseph and announces that "when you hear a dream, you can interpret it" (verse 15). Joseph quickly sets the record straight: "I cannot do it, but God will give Pharaoh the answer he desires" (verse 16).

Once again, Joseph honors God. After hearing the dreams of Pharaoh, Joseph correctly reveals that these are one and the same dream. "God has revealed to Pharaoh what he is about to do" (verse 25). Joseph interprets the dreams as foretelling seven years of plenty followed by seven years of famine. Joseph seals the interpretation by adding even further information in verse 32: "The reason the dream was given to Pharaoh in two forms is that the matter has been firmly decided by God, and God will do it soon."

What must Pharaoh be thinking? Here, he has summoned all the magicians and wise men of Egypt, and none can interpret his dreams. Yet, this Hebrew, this prisoner, is summoned and quickly and decisively interprets the dreams, even telling Pharaoh that God himself is making this known to Pharaoh. Not only does this prisoner interpret the dream, he further instructs the Pharaoh of Egypt as to what he should do during these years of plenty; how he should prepare for the years of famine; how he, the Pharaoh, should rule Egypt! Is this audacity? Is this presumption? Or is this leadership and confidence and faith in one's God?

In view of this young man's knowledge and wisdom, Pharaoh quickly makes a decision—he puts Joseph in charge. Pharaoh summed it up well in verse 38: "Can we find anyone like this man, one in whom is the *spirit of God?*" What a testimony to God, to Joseph's faith, and God's faithfulness.

Thus, Joseph is put in charge. He becomes the leader of the whole land of Egypt, second only to the Pharaoh himself.

Joseph had "waited" thirty years, but during those years he had learned many lessons. He was wise. He was discerning. He was faithful. The dreamer was rewarded, and his wisdom saved not only the people of Egypt but also the people of nearby countries.

The Lesson of Leadership

Good leaders are sometimes hard to find. When one finds a good leader, one will see these qualities: influence, integrity, insight, a team-player, and trust. Leaders know where they are going and how they are going to get there. They "plan their work and work their plan." Joseph was a leader. He had faith in God and the words God had given him.

> Consider it pure joy, my brothers, whenever you face trials of many kinds, because you know that the testing of your faith develops perseverance. Perseverance must finish its work so that you may be mature and complete, not lacking anything. If any of you lacks wisdom, he should ask God, who gives generously to all without finding fault, and it will be given to him.
>
> James 1:2–5

Although it is very difficult to consider trials as "pure joy," the fact remains that we develop perseverance by the testing of our faith. We also need to remember that God gives wisdom to those who ask.

Yes, leaders are born and are made. Our trials have an affect on our leadership abilities, qualifications, and success. Yes, one can "take" leadership, "assume" leadership, and be "assigned" leadership. I believe, however, that true leadership is earned; it is strengthened by learning and by experience. Leaders are respected by their followers, and leaders will train other leaders.

Oh, Lord, may we be ready and willing to take leadership when directed by you. May people see "the spirit of God" in us. May we learn the lessons you teach us so that, when the time comes, we can make a difference in people's lives.

Questions to Ponder ...

- Who do you consider to be a great leader? Why?

- Do you view yourself as a leader? Why or why not?

- Do you think others view you as a leader? Why or why not?

Lesson 50: The Lesson of Honesty

The Dreamer Is Avenged (Genesis 42–44)

This is a long passage, but it contains many illustrations of the importance of honesty—honesty when answering questions, honesty in business affairs, honesty in family relations, and honesty with ourselves.

The writer of Genesis takes us back, once again, to Jacob and his sons, all eleven of whom are still with their father. The sons had grown; they had families of their own, but they very much still respected their father, now up in age. They knew they were loved by their father; but they also knew how much Benjamin, the youngest son, meant to Jacob—and they knew very well the grief and sorrow that had been caused to their father when they had sold Joseph into slavery.

You have been there, have you not, when you wished you had never done a certain act? You know the guilt and pain that can fill your heart. Even though we may be able to "bury" that guilt for a time, sometime, it will make itself known. It is then when we must take an honest look at ourselves and our lives.

For Joseph's brothers, the famine in the land

brought them to this place of honesty. Joseph remembers his dream, and his brothers recognize their punishment.

Who should the brothers meet when they arrive in Egypt to purchase grain? They meet none other than the governor of the land, so they bowed down to him. Even though the brothers did not recognize this man, the brothers were recognized by this man. Joseph remembered his dream; here was the first fulfillment. His brothers were bowing to him. Immediately, he accuses them of being spies. One wonders if this is really what Joseph thought or was this another example of a leadership plan given by God and implemented by Joseph. The brothers are put in custody for three days.

It is interesting to note the word "honest" in this passage. The brothers said they were "honest" men (42:11). They further explain that they are the sons of one man, one son is at home, and one son is "no more."

After the three days, Joseph comes back to this "honest men" issue, and tells the men to leave one brother, return to their father, and bring back the youngest brother with them. The ten sons see this as punishment for what they did to Joseph so many years before. Reuben's "I told you so" statement seals their thoughts and brings tears to Joseph's eyes. Here was the brother who saved him.

Joseph's plan is put into action. Each man's silver is put back in his sack; they load the grain and leave. On the way home, however, they discover their silver returned. Again, they see this as punishment from God.

When they return home, they tell their father what happened, how they were "honest" with the governor, and how Simeon was left behind. Reuben goes so far as to risk his children and his namesake to bring both Simeon and Benjamin back to Jacob. But father Jacob says no. They will not go back to Egypt! He will not risk the loss of yet another son!

However, the famine continues, and more grain is needed for the entire family to live. Judah steps up as leader, reminding Jacob of the words of the Egyptian governor. Judah holds to his honesty and to his integrity. He will accept the blame and the responsibility for whatever happens. The journey must be made.

Jacob sends gifts and double silver in honest payment for both purchases of grain. He sends his sons on their way, praying that God will grant them mercy. Jacob, however, describes himself as "bereaved." The possible loss of yet another son is almost unbearable.

This time their arrival in Egypt finds them taken to the house of the governor instead of imprisoned. This seemed worse to the sons, thinking they would now be made slaves to the governor and none would return home. Again, they are "honest" with the steward, telling him what had happened and how they had returned the silver and brought additional silver with them this time to buy more grain. The steward gives an interesting response in 43:23: "Don't be afraid. Your God, the God of your father, has given you treasure in your sacks." What kind of response was this from an Egyptian?

When Joseph arrives, he is welcomed by bows and gifts. He questions the brothers about their father, and he sees his brother, Benjamin. Overcome with emotion, he hurriedly leaves and weeps.

When the meal is served, everyone is seated by age. Astonishing! Was this a coincidence?

At last, the brothers set out for home, but Joseph has one more lesson to teach. Knowing the "honesty" of these brothers, will they be truthful? Will they stand up for Benjamin and Jacob, or will they abandon Benjamin as they had abandoned him?

The plan is carried out; the brothers are stopped and confronted with the crime. As expected, the brothers are "honest," stating that the guilty person will die and the rest of them will become slaves. Joseph's response is more merciful: the guilty person will be his slave, and the others will go free.

The silver cup is found in Benjamin's sack! Where are these "honest" men now?

All return to Egypt one more time, and Judah begs for mercy. He now realizes that "God has uncovered" their guilt (44:16)—not the guilt of taking the cup or stealing the silver or any of these recent occurrences. This is the guilt of their sin against Joseph so many years before. Judah knows what the loss of Benjamin will mean to his father. Yes, Jacob loves all his sons, but Benjamin and Joseph were the sons of Rachel, Jacob's true love.

The Lesson of Honesty

It appears in this passage, thus far, that honesty was not the best policy. Things only seem to go from bad to worse. Sometimes truth and honesty are very costly. One almost thinks it might be simpler to tell a lie than be honest and tell the truth.

But wait! That kind of logic is totally opposite to every lesson we have discovered thus far. We need to be honest and truthful. God is still sovereign; he is still in control; he will honor our honesty. We do not know "the rest of the story"; we cannot see the whole picture; we do not know what will happen next. But God does!

Oh, Lord, help us to be honest and truthful even if it may seem hopeless and wrong. Help us to trust in you and seek your mercy and grace.

Questions to Ponder ...

- Which is easier, to be honest in business affairs or to be honest in family relations? Why?

- Do you have trouble being honest with yourself? Why or why not?

- How do you respond to truth that hurts (negative truth)? Do you reconcile or retaliate? Can you make a negative truth untrue?

Lesson 51: The Lesson of Forgiveness and Restoration

The Dream Is Fulfilled; The Truth Is Exposed (Genesis 45)

I would have loved to have been there to see Joseph's brothers when Joseph told them who he was. Notice and imagine the responses.

Weeping. Joseph is so overcome at the presence of all his brothers that he wept so loudly that the Egyptians heard him.

Terror. What must have gone through the minds of the brothers?

- *This leader of Egypt told all his attendants to leave; he is alone, and he bursts into tears! What can this mean?*

- *This is Joseph, our brother, the one whom we thought was dead. However, he is alive! Here he is standing before us.*

- *Oh, but wait, the boy we sold into slavery is now a leader in Egypt. Think of the power and author-*

ity he possesses. What will he do to us because of what we did to him?

- *What are we going to tell our father? Will we ever see him again?*

Can you not imagine the scene and these thoughts and fears happening all at once?

Joseph, however, is quick to put his brothers at ease; he is quick to point out to them how God took something meant for evil and turned it into something to be used for good. Joseph's family can come to Egypt; they need not worry about famine, family, homes, possessions. Joseph is in a place of leadership and respect. All of Egypt, with the exception of Pharaoh himself, bows down to, listens to, and obeys Joseph.

I wonder if the brothers now remember those dreams that Joseph had so many years ago—those dreams that sparked their anger and jealousy, those dreams that led them to almost killing but instead selling their brother into slavery. Remember the dreams? The brothers, indeed, have bowed down before their brother, Joseph. Even the "sheaves of grain" in the dreams have been fulfilled in the provision of grain during the famine (37:7). Now the brothers are told to bring their father and all the members of their entire family to Egypt. Ah, yes, even "the sun and moon and eleven stars were bowing down" (37:9) to Joseph now. The dream is fulfilled.

There is more, however, to this passage than the fulfillment of Joseph's dreams. There is forgiveness, there is reconciliation between brothers, and there is restoration of a family and their faith. Once again, the God of Abraham, Isaac, and Jacob has worked in lives and situations in order to accomplish his will. Israel and his family are saved from famine and death. "And we know that in all things God works for the good of those who love him, who have been called according to his purpose" (Romans 8:28).

The Lesson of Forgiveness and Restoration

How do we apply this lesson to our lives? The answer is simply to *believe* in God's forgiveness and his restoration. God welcomes us into his family. He is anxious for us to "return home" to his love and care. He wants to restore our lives and bless us indeed. All we need do is ask—ask for his forgiveness and restoration—and accept—accept his love and plan for our lives.

Oh, Father, where there is need for forgiveness in our lives, may we ask for it. Where we need to forgive, may we do so sincerely. May we see your hands of love and mercy reconciling relationships and restoring people and families. May we remember the lessons in the story of Joseph; and may we remember the promise of Romans 8:28, that in all things you work for our good because we love you and we have been called according to your purpose for our lives.

Questions to Ponder ...

- How does this chapter of Joseph's life compare to the Parable of the Lost Son as recorded in Luke 15:11–32?

- Is there something for which you need to ask forgiveness? Why not now?

- Is there someone you need to forgive? Do so and experience reconciliation and restoration.

The Family Moves to Egypt
(Genesis 46 and 47)

The journey begins with prayer, sacrifices are given, and God speaks to Israel. God, once again, confirms his promise to make Israel into a great nation. The Lord promises to go to Egypt with them and to bring them back again. God also gives Israel the promise that Joseph will close his father's eyes in death.

The Lord has truly been good to Israel. He has been present with him through good times and bad times, through joys and sorrows, through pain and heartache, through peace and blessing. He promises to be with him again in this final journey of his life.

Once in Egypt, Pharaoh keeps his word to Joseph, and the whole family (precisely listed in the Scripture) is settled in the best part of the land, the region of Goshen in the district of Rameses. They were given land for their families, their livestock, and their possessions. They were also given food.

There was no food, however, in Egypt and Canaan. Joseph had collected money from the people for the grain they were buying. When the money ran out, people gave their livestock to Pharaoh in exchange for grain. When the livestock ran out, the Egyptians gave their land and themselves in servitude to Pharaoh. Joseph, however, provided seed for planting, with the understanding that a fifth of the produce was to go to Pharaoh. By the time the famine was over, therefore, Pharaoh owned the Egyptians, all their land, and all their livestock. The Israelites, however, "acquired property, were fruitful, and increased greatly in number" (47:27).

God, indeed, had answered the prayers of Israel and his family. Joseph was found not in a field but in a palace. The family was together, not in Canaan but in Egypt. When the time comes for Israel's death, however, he wants to be buried in the land of his fathers, in the land promised to him by the Lord himself. This prayer, too, will be answered; Joseph gives his word to Israel ... "and Israel worshipped."

The Lesson of Answered Prayer

Oh, to experience the blessing of answered prayer! We know that God answers prayer. Sometimes he says, "no"; sometimes he says, "yes"; sometimes he says, "wait." But he always answers!

God answered Israel's prayers; he granted his requests. We need to realize that God will do the same for us.

Oh, Lord, thank you for the many, many prayers

you have answered on our behalf. Thank you for your presence in all the ups and downs of our lives. Father, thank you, too, for all those prayers that you will answer in the future. Praise your name!

Questions to Ponder ...

- Why do you think some prayers are answered immediately and others take time?

- What prayers has God answered almost immediately in your behalf?

- For what requests are you still awaiting God's response?

Lesson 53: The Lesson of a Father's Blessing

Jacob's Final Years (Genesis 48 and 49)

In this passage, we see the heart of a father and a grandfather. Israel realizes he is about to die, but he rejoices in the blessings of his family. Not only had the Lord restored Joseph to him, but the Lord also allowed him to see his grandsons, the sons of Joseph. Israel must have had a heart full of praise to the Lord! These grandsons are so special to Israel that he includes them as his in the inheritance of the land the Lord will give them. They, too, shall be called by the names of Abraham, Isaac, and Jacob.

Following the Lord's leading, Israel pronounces his blessing upon Ephraim and Manasseh, not in order of birth but in order of blessing and promise. Remember the blessing of Isaac on Jacob and Esau? It is interesting how this blessing, too, goes to the younger rather than the older. God is sovereign. Evidently, it is his will that this blessing be given in this order, and Israel obeys God's direction.

As a final act of love, leadership, and fatherhood, Israel calls his sons before him and tells them what is to come. This he does in the form of a blessing. Can you see and feel Israel's heart as he blesses each son? At first, I read some of these "blessings" more as "curses" or "punishments," but in reading through them again, I see a father who knows his sons. Israel knows the strengths and weaknesses of each son. He compares them to animals that those strengths may be better understood and recognized. Judah will be the leader of the Israelites, not Joseph as expected. Joseph, however, receives a bountiful blessing in proportion to his part in saving the family through the work of the Almighty God.

The Lesson of a Father's Blessing—This lesson is summed up in Genesis 49:28 and 33:

> All these are the twelve tribes of Israel, and this is what their father said to them when he blessed them, giving each the blessing appropriate to him ... When Jacob had finished giving instructions, he drew his feet up into the bed, breathed his last and was gathered to his people.

These were a father's final words to his sons— words of truth, words of advice, words of love, and words of blessing.

The Lesson of a Father's Blessing

In today's society we do not hear much about a father's final blessing given to his children. This seems sad.

Perhaps this is a custom that we should adopt. We leave final wills and testaments wherein family members may be named or described. Perhaps we need to encourage and edify our children one last time before we die. Our blessings may not be like those of Israel, but they can be personal and special to our family. Blessing our children and encouraging them in their faith, however, should not be put off. We need to affirm our children every chance we get.

Oh, Lord, thank you for this lesson of a father's blessing. May we, as parents, know and love our children. May we recognize their strengths and their talents. May we teach them your ways, and may we bless their lives not only in words but also in actions. In your name, our Father in heaven, we pray. Amen.

Questions to Ponder ...

- Do you know of people who give blessings to their children when they are born? How is this done and what is said?

- If you were to pronounce a blessing upon your children, what would you say?

The Burial of Jacob; The Death of Joseph (Genesis 50)

This passage gives us a glimpse of the respect that Pharaoh, his officials, and all of Egypt had for Joseph. At the loss of his father, all Egypt mourned with him; for seventy days, they mourned with him. Their love and respect for Joseph went beyond the land of Egypt, for the "dignitaries of Egypt" accompanied Joseph and his family to Canaan to bury his father. Verse 9b tells us, that it was a "very large company" who went with him. Joseph was truly respected by the people of Egypt.

Thus, Joseph's promise to his father was fulfilled. Jacob was buried with his forefathers, Abraham and Isaac. And a legacy was passed on.

Joseph and his brothers and family continued to live in Egypt in peace and forgiveness. Joseph, too, was blessed with a long life and "saw the third generation of Ephraim's children ... also the children of Makir son of Manasseh" (verse 23). However, sensing his oncoming death, he too addressed his brothers. It is interesting to note that Joseph told his brothers that "God will surely come to your aid and take you up out of this land to the land he promised on oath to Abraham, Isaac, and Jacob" (verse 24). A second time, he tells them, "God will surely come to your aid" (verse 25), but here he also asks his brothers to swear an oath: "Then you must carry my bones up from this place." His brothers agreed. When Joseph died, he was embalmed and placed in a coffin in Egypt.

. . .

At this point, we come to not only the end of the Book of Genesis but also the end of the history of the Israelites, the Hebrews, at least for a long period of time. (The Book of Exodus begins approximately four hundred years later.)

The Israelites are left with a legacy of faith in God as shown to them by their forefathers. A legacy is something handed down from an ancestor. It can be a heritage, property inherited, a tradition, or a status acquired through birth.

Here, the family of Joseph has received a legacy of faith. They have a promise from the Lord God of a land they are to inhabit. They have lessons learned by their forefathers. They are descendants of Abraham, Isaac, and Jacob. The legacy left them by Jacob and Joseph is a great legacy, one to be treasured and one to be remembered.

The Lesson of Leaving a Legacy

How can anyone leave a lesson better than a legacy of faith in God? There is nothing more important than this to pass to our children. To know the Lord, God Almighty, to trust him, to follow him, to love him—there is no greater legacy. Once more, we come back to lesson one: God is sovereign. He knows our todays and our tomorrows. He made us; therefore, he knows what is best for us. He knows our strengths and our weaknesses. He knows our comings and our goings. He loves us, even as we are, and wants the very best for us.

Oh, Lord, may we remember that you are God, the God of the universe, and the God of our very soul. Help us to stay true to you and pass on a legacy of faith to our children and grandchildren and to those with whom we come in contact. Bless us, Lord, and help us be blessings to others. In your name, we pray. Amen.

Questions to Ponder...

- How would you define a legacy?
- What legacy will you leave to your children or those you know?

Heritage, Take Two (Genesis 10)

Has God ever directed you to go back and read a Scripture again? When reading the same passage you have read before, did you ever see something new? Yes, of course. This happens all the time because God's Word is alive and speaks to us differently at different times.

In this instance, after completing this study of the Book of Genesis, God sent me back for "a second look" at this particular passage.

The previous time I studied it, God pointed out to me the importance of heritage. The second time, he pointed out the importance of history.

In this very important chapter, the writer of Genesis gives us the history of the habitation of the world after the flood. Here we see the three sons of Noah and how their descendants populated the "new earth." Yes, we see some different "ites" of people, but we also learn information about these people and where they settled.

First, let us look at the sons of Japheth. We learn that some of Japheth's descendants were maritime people (verse 5). They settled close to the seas (Mediterranean, Adriatic, Aegean, Black, and Caspian Seas). They were probably fishermen and/or businessmen who set up trade centers at these seaports for commerce. Notice the names of these sons. These names and locations are mentioned throughout the Bible. I noticed Tarshish. Could this be the home of the Apostle Paul (Saul of Tarsus) we read about in the New Testament?

Next, we meet the sons of Ham. We learn quite a bit about these sons and descendants. Cush's son, Nimrod, was a mighty warrior and hunter (verses 8–9). Places are identified: cities like Babylon and Nineveh, countries of Canaan and Assyria. Their descendants most likely settled in Egypt, Ethiopia, the northern part of Africa, and, of course, Canaan. Again, these are names that one reads throughout the Scriptures.

Finally, we meet the descendants of Shem. We are not given a lot of detail here, but we are told that the region where they lived stretched to "the eastern hill country" (verse 30). These were the Semitic peoples, the ancestors of Abraham, Isaac, and Jacob, the ancestors of Joseph, the lineage of the Israelites.

The Lesson of a Second Look

The nations of Noah, the repopulation of the earth after the flood, a new beginning for mankind—this second look shows the importance of history, mankind's history, our history. The Lesson of a Second Look also points out the lesson of studying God's

Word, the Bible. It is a living book filled with many, many lessons for us to learn. Depending on our needs and circumstances at the time, we will see new lessons, new hopes, new assurance, new grace, new mercy— new lessons every time we read and study God's Word.

Oh, Lord, thank you for directing us back for a "Second Look" at this particular passage. Even though we have read this Book of Genesis many times, we gleaned new lessons and new insights. May we always find your Word fresh, alive, and meaningful in our lives. Amen and Amen.

Questions to Ponder ...

- Have you ever read a Scripture and gained one insight then read it again later and gained a new insight? Share with someone that example and the Lesson of a Second Look.

- Why do you think the Bible is considered the "living Word" of God?

Final Thoughts

This book started out as a journal I wrote while studying the Book of Genesis. I wanted to specifically look for lessons that God was trying to teach the people in this book of history.

However, I found so much more. I found that sometimes lessons would practically "jump off the page." Most times, however, I found I had to read and reread and maybe even read again before I saw the lesson God was trying to teach me. I also noticed that lesson one kept reappearing throughout the Scripture. Maybe that is because we all need to work on that lesson the most.

Lessons learned? No, they are all lessons to be learned, but the actual learning takes time and practice. Some lessons will take more time and practice than others. Since we are all still here, we have not yet reached perfection. Thus, we are continuing to learn. As Romans 12:2 says,

> Do not conform any longer to the pattern of this world, but be transformed by the *renewing* of your mind. Then you will be able to test and approve what God's will is—his good, pleasing and perfect will.

The Book of Genesis is not a book telling us in detail about the creation of the earth. It is a book telling us in detail about the formation of a people, God's people. This book tells us how God's people were molded, shaped, and formed. It shows us how God moved in people's lives then, and it helps us realize that he continues to move in people's lives today, doing it his way.

. . .

Oh, Lord, thank you for this study of your Word. Thank you for speaking to us through these valuable lessons. Help us to remember them and apply them to our lives. If we can remember only one, Lord, help it to be the first and last one—you are sovereign. You are in charge, and you will work everything out for our good. We praise thee, oh, Lord. Amen.

listen|imagine|view|experience

AUDIO BOOK DOWNLOAD INCLUDED WITH THIS BOOK!

In your hands you hold a complete digital entertainment package. Besides purchasing the paper version of this book, this book includes a free download of the audio version of this book. Simply use the code listed below when visiting our website. Once downloaded to your computer, you can listen to the book through your computer's speakers, burn it to an audio CD or save the file to your portable music device (such as Apple's popular iPod) and listen on the go!

How to get your free audio book digital download:

1. Visit www.tatepublishing.com and click on the e|LIVE logo on the home page.
2. Enter the following coupon code:
   fc0d-2236-cfc0-70ee-8065-d1f0-4579-07f7
3. Download the audio book from your e|LIVE digital locker and begin enjoying your new digital entertainment package today!